MW00715973

CALLING THE MARITIMES HOME

Origins, Attitudes, Quirks & Curiosities

Julie V. Watson

RAINCOAST BOOKS

Vancouver

Copyright © 1998 by Julie V. Watson

All rights reserved. No part of this publication may be reproduced or transmitted in any form or by any means, electronic or mechanical, including photocopying, recording or by any information storage and retrieval system, now known or to be invented, without permission in writing from the publisher.

First published in 1998 by

Raincoast Books
8680 Cambie Street
Vancouver, B.C.
V6P 6M9
(604) 323-7100

Visit our Web Site: www.raincoast.com

1 2 3 4 5 6 7 8 9 10

CANADIAN CATALOGUING IN PUBLICATION DATA

Watson, Julie V., 1943-
Calling the Maritimes home

isbn 1-55192-149-9

1. Maritime Provinces. I. Title.

fc2025.5.w37 1998   971.5'04   c97-910977-9
f1035.8.w37 1998

Printed in Canada

THE CANADA COUNCIL | LE CONSEIL DES ARTS
FOR THE ARTS | DU CANADA
SINCE 1957 | DEPUIS 1957

Raincoast Books gratefully acknowledges the support of the Government of Canada, through the Book Publishing Industry Development Program, the Canada Council for the Arts and the Department of Canadian Heritage. We also acknowledge the assistance of the Province of British Columbia, through the British Columbia Arts Council.

CONTENTS

DEDICATION

For my sister-in-pal Sue
who in her passing strengthened
my appreciation for life and
belief in living for now

And my sister-in-pal Patricia
who keeps the link alive and well

For Jack and For John as always
and the new light in my life – Tipsy

THE BEGINNING

When my phone rang and a gentleman by the name of Mark Stanton introduced himself as the publisher of Raincoast Books, then asked if I would be interested in writing a book to be titled, "Calling the Maritimes Home," my mind went blank. Just for a few seconds. Then ideas began to flash in, one after another, changing the void to a mass of excitement and dare I say inspiration!

I couldn't get the yes out fast enough!

Keep in mind that this is not the way books usually get written. Normally, the author comes up with an idea, spends months refining it, pitching it and negotiating a contract. By the time the writing begins the project has lost its edge. Not this one.

This was a gem, a gift. My first thoughts included, "what a neat idea, why didn't I think of that!" Well, I didn't but Raincoast did – so we happily formed a union. Almost before I had time to answer myself, I was happily writing!

Mark, an expatriate Maritimer himself, had some, "Make sure you include…" suggestions and a plan of sorts for the book, but he had the courage to turn me loose and wait and see what I came up with. And so began one of the more difficult tasks I've faced. Deciding what to include and what to set aside! We have already, laughingly at this point, talked of a volume two.

The research and writing have been such fun! I've visited museums, archives, libraries, historic sites; interviewed and questioned; followed leads and developed a passionate appreciation for the Maritimes.

Not that I didn't have one before, but even I, an avid reader, researcher and ponderer – yes I'm one of those people who takes the time to read a historic marker or plaque, then stare off into space as my mind creates images of what I've just read – have been amazed at facts I discovered.

So, when asked what *Calling the Maritimes Home* is all about, I reply that it contains snippets of fact and fancy that will make the reader constantly utter, "I didn't know that!" And I pose a few questions:

What did privateers have to do with some of Canada's major banks?
Where was Nova Scotia before it moved to the Maritimes?
What happened when a seaweed mutated?
And what was Artillery Punch anyhow? Or Mothers Milk?
Where did Canada's first movie, theatre, and novel originate?
What is the oldest written language in North America?
Is "hugger-in-the-buff" an amorous naked chap or something to eat?

Maritimers of years ago counted among their number privateers, pirates, female spies and slavers; there were blacksmiths, cabinetmakers and soapmakers; as well as healers, soldiers and artisans. Settlers, both women and men, were "jacks-of-all-trades." They had to be "handy" to survive, to be adaptable to cope with living so much at the whim of weather and Mother Nature. Women often had dual roles running the family and the business, even if it meant taking up arms. Throughout it all, if we borrow a modern description, they had to learn to not sweat the small stuff.

Life was often harsh and full of things needing to be done. Even so, Maritimers always had time for a bit of fun. Sometimes it was a get – together over work; a fulling party or a barn raising would be followed by a glorious feast and dance. A card play, a shower, a sophisticated ball, a feast, a ceilidh, a kitchen party or a lobster boil or clam bake on the beach – simply excuses for bringing people together. It's the folks that count.

We haven't totally dwelled in the past – some of this book is very today. But what has gone before is undoubtedly its essence. Like many scraps of fabric that come together to form a quilt, or building blocks that become a building, *Calling the Maritimes Home* takes many small parts and turns them into what we hope you'll agree is a good read.

It is fascinating to see how things began. It's equally gratifying to see how many of those traits exhibited by early Maritimers are still part of our "community" today. Read on for my version of just what it is that makes other Canadians look east with just a little pang of… what, could that be envy?

Home's not merely four square walls,
  Though with pictures hung and gilded;
Home is where affection calls,
  Fill'd with shrines the heart hath builded.

Home's not merely roof and room,
  It needs something to endear it;
Home is where the heart can bloom,
  Where's there's some kind lip to cheer it.

What is home with none to meet,
  None to welcome, nor to greet us?
Home is sweet, and only sweet
  Where there's one we love to meet us.

Author Unknown
The Maritime School Series,
Third Reading Book

Chapter 1

Where We Came From

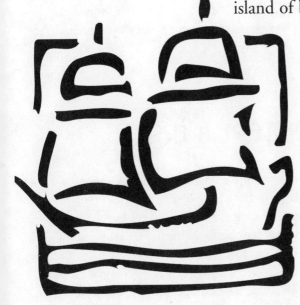

A Mi'kmaq woman dreamed one night that a small island floated toward the land of Nagooset. The island contained garments of white rabbit skins at one glance – then it became an island of bare trees with black bars on its branches. The woman told her dreams to the elders and vision people of the village, but no one at the time could interpret the significance of what the dream meant. With the sighting of the first European sailing ships, the vision of the Mi'kmaq prophet became clear.

- Traditional Mi'kmaq legend

Truth be told, the European discovery of the Maritimes was a mistake. Explorers were looking for China, seeking the wealth of Cathay described by Marco Polo, who had made the long trek across Asia to China in the 13th century. Its riches were the bait that lured Christopher Columbus across the Atlantic in 1492, John Cabot in 1497 and Jacques Cartier in 1534. Columbus claimed the West Indies for Spain, while Cartier planted a cross for France on the Gaspé shore, excitedly anticipating that the St. Lawrence River would offer a route to the East. Cabot landed in the Maritimes, probably at Cape Breton – although Newfoundlanders swear otherwise – and claimed it for England.

But he was not the first European to wash up on our shores. Some speculate that the Norseman Leif Ericsson landed 500 years earlier in Nova Scotia and Newfoundland. Leif had likely never heard of China. He simply blew off course while sailing between Iceland and Greenland. While this lot were bumbling about making discoveries by accident, humble European fishermen from countries such as Spain and Portugal regularly commuted back and forth in search of the noble codfish. Going ashore to dry and salt their wondrous catches before travelling back home, chances are they encountered the real first Maritimers, the Micmac (a.k.a. Mi'kmaq) and Malecite (a.k.a. Maliseet).

WHO GOT HERE FIRST?

First Nations people have lived in the Maritimes for more than ten millennia. Hunting implements from a caribou hunting camp occupied 6,000 years before the building of the pyramids of Egypt are on display at Nova Scotia's Museum of Natural History. Isolated finds of fluted-stone spear tips confirm that "Paleo Natives," as they are called, were in the Maritimes region 11,000 years ago. A known habitation site, at Debert, Nova Scotia, is one of the most important finds of this period in eastern North America.

The Micmac were our earliest connoisseurs, feasting on oysters just like people do today. One of their largest camps was at Malpeque, Prince Edward Island, an area that became so famous for its oysters they are known as Malpeques around the world. The first white settlers found the shores of the Darnley River lined with enormous piles of oyster shells, left from days of feasting.

Chief Membertou (1505-1610), the most famous Micmac chief in history, was invaluable to Cartier in 1534 and to Champlain in 1605.

By the time Port-Royal was established by the French fur trader and explorer Samuel de Champlain in 1605, there had been a long period of contact between the Micmac and Malecite and those enterprising fishermen from Europe. Furs and hides had been exchanged for European goods, which had replaced traditional tools. Around this time, these trade goods start showing up in native burials. The largest and most distinctive was the copper cooking pot; thus, the graves became known as "copper kettle" burial sites.

For hundreds of years, non-Natives spelled the name of the Micmac thus. In recent years, there has been a move afoot to use the spelling that the Micmac themselves use – that is, Mi'kmaq. As a writer, I was uncertain which spelling to adopt, so I approached some friends who live on the Lennox Island Reserve on Prince Edward Island and asked them which version is correct. They felt that the use of Mi'kmaq belongs to their nation, and preferred that I continue to use Micmac unless I am transcribing the name from a Micmac person. I respect their wishes. That is why you will find two spellings used in this book.

The Micmac called Prince Edward Island Abegweit, meaning "cradled on the waves." According to legend, Glooscap, their mythological hero, gave the island its bright red soil. He wanted a cheerful place where he could go when he wished for a holiday, so he took his paintbrush and coloured the rocks and earth red – the most cheerful of colours. He did good!

An important Malecite village or fortress was built at what we now know as Meductic, downriver from Woodstock, New Brunswick. War parties often passed along the St. John River, a main route between Acadia and New England, and it was necessary to guard the village against the Mohawks. Excavations have turned up artifacts and details about the fort and its dimensions. It was at this fort that nine-year-old John Gyles was kidnaped and held captive for six years in the early days of settlement. The son of a New England judge, he was the first English-speaking resident of New Brunswick. New Brunswick writer-historian Stuart Trueman used the diaries of Gyles to write *The Ordeal of John Gyles*, a book about the incident.

ACADIA: PARADISE LOST

Samuel de Champlain and Sieur Pierre du Gua de Monts, general roustabouts and adventurers, were sent to the New World by merchants who had won the fur concession of the Gulf of St. Lawrence from the king of France. The rough, unproven land where they were sent was known by the French as *Acadie,* Acadia in English, named after a legendary area in Ancient Greece that had become synonymous for bucolic beauty. Shows the optimism typical of today's real estate industry was alive even then! Champlain and de Monts established Canada's first colony at Port-Royal (now Annapolis Royal) in the Bay of Fundy in 1604-05, where the first dwellings were built and crops grown, before paddling off to the interior in search of beaver pelts and other riches. The first settlements didn't stick – bad weather and isolation sent the settlers packing. After a couple of false starts, though, a permanent French settlement was finally established.

Explorers and fur traders played their part, but their era passed, and it was the settlers who built the foundation of the Maritimes. They were the first Europeans to dig in and stay – to build homes, develop communities and establish a Maritime way of life. The Micmac helped the first Acadian settlers to adapt to new lands and new foods, such as maple syrup and fiddleheads. Their own way of life was disrupted and forever changed, yet they generously aided the newcomers.

Often ignored by Mother France, the Acadians went about establishing a prosperous agricultural community. They dyked and improved the rich farmlands around the bay. They traded with the English colonies to the south for things they could not grow.

The farmers and labourers who came to the New World in the mid-17th century, most from central western France, began a new life in Acadie. Strong family ties and a common religion, language and ancestral tradition helped to create an independent, cohesive society. As the population grew, they began to settle farther up the Annapolis River and, by the end of the century, along the Fundy shore. Today Acadian communities can be found in all three Maritime provinces.

But paradise was shortlived. Acadia was soon caught up in the global strife between Britain and France.

Over the next century, Britain and France, constantly bickering, passed Acadia back and forth between them like a hot Spud Island potato. Finally, by the mid-18th century, Britain had gained the upper hand. The British governor, Charles Lawrence, did not believe that the Acadians would remain neutral. Nor did he want to send them to Louisbourg, Île St. Jean (as the French called Prince Edward Island) or Quebec to strengthen the French settlements there. Without informing Britain of his plan, in 1755 he schemed with the governor of Massachusetts to scatter the Acadians throughout the 13 colonies of what is now the United States.

The largest Danish colony in North America (125+ years old) is in New Denmark, N.B.

Men, women and children were expelled. As part of the deportation, two shiploads were sent to France but were refused permission to land. The Acadians settled along the American Atlantic seaboard. Some escaped deportation by fleeing to the woods, finding refuge at Quebec or Île St. Jean or making their way to Louisiana, where they became known as Cajuns. A caravan of over 700, referred to as "The Heroic Ones," walked 600 miles to make homes in New Brunswick.

Of the 10,000 Acadians estimated to have been living in Nova Scotia, it is believed that 8,000 were taken away, their homes destroyed. Some fled to the French settlement on Île St. Jean. The influx of newcomers to that colony, estimated to be 2,000 individuals, coupled with a lack of housing, clothing and supplies, severely taxed everyone. Crops in 1756 and 1757 were poor. Many of the older people were taken to Quebec, where it was thought that life would be easier. When the French surrendered at Louisbourg, they also gave up Île St. Jean, agreeing that all settlers from that colony should be sent back to France. About 4,600 people on the island begged to be allowed to stay. They had not taken up arms against the British. A petition was taken to Louisbourg, but it was refused. Many fled to New Brunswick and Quebec. Some went to the islands of St. Pierre and Miquelon in the Gulf of St. Lawrence. Others were sent to France. About 300 remained on the island and eventually took the oath of allegiance to the British king.

Those determined individuals who stayed, along with those who trickled back after the deportation, are the ancestors of today's Acadians.

 *One of the oldest churches in Acadia (1679) is on the island of La Valour. The burial ground is across the river, necessitating a custom of holding all funerals at low tide.*

A flag made by Marie Babineau, a schoolteacher at St. Louis, Kent County, New Brunswick, adopted by Acadians as their official banner in the early 1880s, can be seen at the University of Moncton's Acadian Museum. The striking flag – the blue, white and red flag of France with a gold star on the blue portion – has distinguished Acadians from French Canadians in Quebec. Acadians also have their own hymn, "Ave Marie Stella," sung in Latin on a special holiday, the Feast of the Assumption, celebrated on 15 August.

During the years of their exodus, wandering Acadian couples seldom saw a priest, so church marriages did not take place. A Nova Scotia parish register bears this entry by the priest: "Today, I married a couple in the presence of their grown children."

LOUISBOURG:
CANADA'S GIBRALTAR

Starting as a simple codfishing town, Louisbourg grew to be the greatest French fortress on the coast of Acadie. For a quarter century, starting in 1719, fortifications were built up, girdling the town with a thick stone wall. Inside the wall were a governor's palace, barracks, houses, taverns, meeting places, several churches, a hospital, arsenals and warehouses. Louisbourg became a symbol of French might in the New World.

In 1745, during a time when Britain and France were at war, a force of New Englanders, supported by the British, captured Louisbourg from the French. At the end of the war, they gave it back and the French rebuilt, making Louisbourg stronger than ever.

By 1757, Britain and France were at war once again. Couldn't they learn to behave themselves! British troops had begun to assemble in Halifax to train for an assault on Louisbourg. As he knew that the French had more warships and more soldiers, the British commander refused to do battle, keeping his troops busy gardening instead. After all, fresh vegetables were known to prevent scurvy. They became known as the "cabbage-planting expedition."

In 1758 a stronger British force arrived in Halifax. General Amherst commanded about 11,000 soldiers. Admiral Boscawen had a strong fleet of about 40 warships and more than 12,000 men. At the end of May, the whole force sailed to Louisbourg, confident that this time they were stronger than the French.

But the French had known for a long time that the British were coming, and they had prepared well. Governor Drucour had 8,000 men and 800 guns. Knowing that he was outnumbered, he set out to delay the British as long as possible, believing that to do so would keep Quebec and New France safe for another year. The French fought bravely, but gradually the big British guns battered the fortifications.

With huge holes in the wall, most of the town in ruins and only four guns still able to fire, Drucour gave up. After a siege of seven weeks, the French surrendered for the second and last time.

All over the British Empire, people rejoiced when they heard about the fall of Louisbourg. Bells rang and bonfires burned in Halifax and Boston. Returning soldiers and sailors were fêted.

After moving on to capture Quebec, the British returned to Louisbourg and reduced the huge stone citadel to ruins. Sailors and soldiers worked for months blowing up the walls and fortifications. Finally, the fortress lay in dust and ruins, as did French power in North America.

In the 1960s, reconstruction of the fortress began. Today it is the masterpiece in Parks Canada's portfolio, with costumed animators, reenactments and museums.

LOYAL TO THE CROWN

By the Peace of Paris in 1763, practically all of North America "belonged" to Britain, and it was a solidly Anglo-Saxon empire. Yet, within a few years, all but a handful of settlers to the south would rebel and declare their independence. French Quebec and predominantly English-speaking Nova Scotia (as the combined territory of what is now the Maritimes was then known) remained in the empire and provided a refuge for those in the American colonies who did not join the revolt.

The coming of some 50,000 to 60,000 United Empire Loyalists changed the face of Canada almost overnight. They upped the population by 50 percent, necessitating the creation of two new provinces, New Brunswick and Upper Canada (now Ontario), within 15 years. The Loyalists brought a great burst of energy and ideas for the expansion of the country. They had a political heritage that was new: the right of private citizens to control their own affairs.

The British provided free land, clothing, food and lumber, giving Loyalists a start in the Maritimes. They settled whole new areas in the valley of the St. John River, near the Bay of Fundy and in Shelburne, Nova Scotia. The world's largest single migration of English people took place in 1783 when 10,000 Loyalists evacuated from New York to Shelburne, making it, for a time, North America's 4th largest city.

Tales abound about Loyalists living in tents or roughly built cabins. Used to a milder climate, they suffered through their first winter, with few necessities and often with useless luxuries they had carried with them. Damask table covers, silver plates, finely crafted furniture, these did little to alleviate hunger or ward off the cold. How frustrating it must have been surrounded by costly goods while sleeping on boughs or rough mattresses woven of bark. Thanks in great part to the assistance of Native people, who provided meat and taught the newcomers how to live off the land, most Loyalists survived that first winter.

> "I climbed up the hill, watching the sails disappearing. Such loneliness came over me. Although I had not shed a tear through the war, I sat down on the damp moss with my baby held tight, and cried."
> – *Loyalist grandmother of Sir Samuel Leonard Tilley, lieutenant-governor of New Brunswick, about 1784*

The first Canadian almanac, the Nova Scotia Calendar, was published in 1770.

The Loyalists were prime settlers. Loyal to the crown, they were committed to improving their lot and had the experience and knowledge to do it. Loyalist women were resourceful and strong of mind and body. One hid her fiancé under her petticoats to save him from capture by the revolutionaries. Another used her petticoats to carry a fortune in silver past a checkpoint. Disguised as being very pregnant, she must have experienced tense moments as she trudged past revolutionaries who gallantly stepped aside in respect for her "delicate condition." Another, Dorothy Kendrick, was the talk of the St. John River in 1769 after she gave birth to twins in a canoe. And Mrs. John Glennie, the fiery wife of a member of New Brunswick's first legislature, swore that if her husband had not challenged a certain gentleman to a duel she would have done so herself and treated him far more severely.

Women saved Chester, Nova Scotia, from the invading Yankee navy in 1782. By reversing their skirts, which were lined with red material, they appeared to be British soldiers – redcoats.

YANKEE CONNECTIONS

If the Americans had played their cards right they may well have included eastern Canada in their nation. By 1776 there were about 20,000 whites in Nova Scotia. (Remember, this was the three modern provinces.) Most were not openly loyal to Britain. In fact it was only the couple of thousand in Halifax who depended on the Royal Navy for income who had close ties to the Motherland. The Yanks themselves changed those attitudes.

First a Yankee farmer led an attack on Fort Cumberland near the now New Brunswick/Nova Scotia border and had to be routed out by the Royal Navy. Then American privateers looted Charlottetown and kidnaped the governor. Ports were raided and folks began to get just a little tired of it all.

Evangelist Henry Alline, a Puritan, began tramping the roads, arousing anti-American feelings at his revival meetings. He preached that God had led His faithful to Nova Scotia, which he called the "Apple of his eye," where the church would be reborn. Alline, a strong orator, took advantage of the already undermined ties with New England, to offer a new identity and draw together the people of Nova Scotia.

The ties between what is now the United States and Nova Scotia were many:

- Yankee patriot Paul Revere lived near Yarmouth in 1772.
- Nova Scotia rebels did briefly hoist the 'Stars and Stripes' over Halifax.
- George Washington is reported to have said his greatest regret was not assisting Nova Scotia's Revolutionaries in 1776.
- Inventor Thomas Edison's Loyalist grandfather was the town planner for Digby, Nova Scotia, in 1773.

- A New England delegation to Nova Scotia proposed that New England secede and join Nova Scotia in 1812.
- The son of Benedict Arnold, traitor to the Americans but hero to the English, designed the initial plans for Halifax's famous Citadel Fort in 1818.

After defecting from the American Revolution, Benedict Arnold fled to New Brunswick. In Fredericton he immediately made enemies by forcing a sterling member of the community into bankruptcy. In 1787, acknowledging that he was not welcome in Fredericton, he and his wife packed and left for Saint John. Branded as a turncoat, Arnold was never trusted. His store burned, and his partner accused him of setting the fire himself to collect the insurance. Arnold sued his accuser, but it appeared the judge didn't particularly like him either. He was awarded 20 shillings in damages. His overbearing manner and his reputation for dishonesty did little to win friends. On one occasion, he was burned in effigy in front of his home, a sign reading "traitor." Arnold left town in the boat for which some said he never paid. He later said of his Saint John experience, "It was a shipwreck from which I have escaped."

OF KILTS & PIPES

When the English heard of the French settlements in Acadia, and the wealth in furs, they recalled the voyages of John Cabot and decided that the English had more right to the territory than the French. James I of England was eager for the increase in wealth and power that new colonies would generate. At the same time, Sir William Alexander of Scotland thought that, because there was already a New England, a New Spain, a New Netherlands and a New France, there should be a New Scotland as well. James I gave a charter to Sir William in 1621 granting him all of New Scotland – basically, the Maritimes – the land already occupied by the French. An oversight or a provocation? Hard to say.

It was not easy to get people to emigrate to New Scotland (or Nova Scotia as it came to be known, using the latin version), and the first voyage proved disastrous, landing in Newfoundland, where all but 10 newcomers perished in the winter. The next voyage was more successful, but Sir William had run out of money. To raise capital, he convinced James I to sell titles. Any Scottish gentleman could be a knight baronet of Nova Scotia if he paid a fee to Sir William, who would use the money to form a colony.

Part of the yard of Edinburgh Castle is part of Nova Scotia. This strange fact is connected with Sir William's sale of titles. A man could not become a knight baronet of Nova Scotia unless he stood on Nova Scotian soil while the king touched him on the shoulder with a sword. The king was not about to take the long and arduous voyage, so he designated a plot of land within the walls of Edinburgh Castle as part of Nova Scotia – as it remains to this day. Descendants of the baronets are quite proud of their ancestors' title.

The first Scots in Cape Breton were set upon by the French in 1629. Those who survived the attack and a voyage back across the Atlantic as poorly treated prisoners landed on the English coast, thus ending the first Scottish settlement of Cape Breton. Others settled at Port-Royal, which the French had abandoned. That colony flourished, but in 1632 the Scots were again forced out by the French. These early Scots left a legacy that still makes us proud: the flag of Nova Scotia, the coat of arms and the name of the province.

The first permanent settlement of Scottish Highlanders on Prince Edward Island was established in 1770. Depending on which books you read, it was either members of the Fraser clan from Ross, Inverness, Sutherland and Argyll in Scotland who sailed on the *Falmouth* or 60 families from Argyllshire who believed they were going to the Carolinas on board the *Annabella,* which wrecked when it ran aground on St. John's Island, which was separated in 1769 after colonists there petitioned England to make their island a colony separate from Nova Scotia. Sir Walter Patterson, an Irishman, was appointed governor. When he arrived in 1770, there were only 150 families and five proprietors living on the island.

The *Hector* arrived in Pictou in 1773 carrying almost 200 Scots eager to settle New Scotland, thus beginning a large-scale emigration to eastern Nova Scotia.

Near Montague, Prince Edward Island, in the Brudenell River Park, lies a tiny island that typifies in its quiet way the ties of the New World with the Old World. Crossing a small causeway, one comes to a set of sturdy but worn steps leading to a magical trail through the woods that ends in what the Scots would describe as a 'wee glen.' Here lies a monument marking the graves of Donald Gordon, patriarch of the Brudenell Gordons, and Christina MacLaren, daughter of James MacLaren, patriarch of the Brudenell MacLarens. Both were born in Toncastle, Scotland, he in 1762, she in 1776. They married in 1796 and emigrated to Brudenell in 1803. She died in 1804 at the age of 28 years. He died in 1819, at 57 years of age. His father, Daniel Gordon, of Georgetown, built numerous ships. Donald's brother, Alexander, was an officer in the English army and fought in the American Revolution.

THE MUCH-TRAVELLED SCOTS OF ST. ANN'S

Norman MacLeod grew up and studied religion at a turbulent time in Scotland. A strict Calvinist, he quickly found disfavour with the Church of Scotland, whose influence even drove him from a teaching career. MacLeod returned to his old career as a fisherman, preaching regularly to what had become a large following. The church continued to persecute him, driving him to consider emigration. In July 1817, leaving his wife and children behind, he boarded the barque *Frances Ann* bound for Pictou, Nova Scotia.

Landing at Pictou, the immigrants encountered a booming frontier town unlike anything they had ever known – lumber was king, and rum flowed endlessly from the West Indies. There were few restrictions and plenty of money, and hard drinking was the rule. Settlers had to take scattered lots of land even though they wished to stay together. The strong arm of the church could still be felt. Even though family and friends joined MacLeod, Pictou was not the land of their dreams.

After two years, a settlement of Highlanders in Ohio invited MacLeod to be their minister. He and his flock built a ship, derisively dubbed "The Ark" by the people of Pictou, and set sail. The plan was to go up around Cape Breton and then down around Florida into the Mississippi to sail up to Ohio. Sailing along the coast of Cape Breton to test the ship before facing the turbulent Atlantic Ocean, they stopped one sunny afternoon at St. Ann's Harbour. The next day, they sailed through the circle of mountains to the head of the bay. The waters were teeming with fish. They landed, deliberated and decided to stay.

Cape Breton Island is home to the world's largest population of Scots outside Scotland.

By 1848 the settlement, over 25 years old, had matured, and business, religion and education were well established. But disaster struck: crops failed, MacLeod had alienated himself from other clergy who might have offered help. Starvation was upon them.

In the spring of 1849, MacLeod's son wrote urging his father to join him in Australia. Norman was on the move again, taking many of his flock with him. They built the *Margaret* and finally set sail in 1851 with 140 people aboard for a 167-day voyage to Adelaide, Australia, then on to Melbourne. But Norman encountered another boom town, and life proved very difficult. So in 1853 he sailed once more, this time to New Zealand, and began a settlement at Waipu. Six ships and over 800 souls followed him. Most of them settled in New Zealand, leaving St. Ann's much changed and many families divided by 12,000 miles.

The story does not end there. Today a collection of oil paintings and ink drawings depicting Reverend MacLeod's life is on display at the Gaelic College of Celtic Arts and Crafts in St. Ann's. And in 1990 the people of New Zealand, celebrating their 150th birthday as a nation, sought out the people of Victoria County, Nova Scotia, and formed the St. Ann's/Baddeck/Waipu Twinning Society to foster cultural, educational and friendly exchanges. Nice to know that the families keep in touch!

OUR FAIR CITIES

Halifax was founded after Louisbourg was returned to France by the 1748 Treaty of Utrecht. New Englanders were furious, so Britain agreed to build a town between the two locations. The place chosen was Chebucto, known as a fine harbour for ships, easily defended and able to shelter the whole British navy. Governor Edward Cornwallis was sent to found the town, and he was followed by 13 ships with over 2,500 settlers. They were stunned to discover forest down to the water's edge. Not a single cleared space could be seen. Haligonians built their town in the wilderness while living on board the ship. It was a slow job – no bulldozers for this crew. While the settlers toiled to create a town, soldiers worked above them to fortify Citadel Hill to prevent enemies from hauling guns up it in wartime and firing down on the town. Eventually, the settlers tired of the backbreaking work and sat down on the job – literally. They refused to work anymore unless paid. Perhaps theirs was the first strike in Canada.

Saint John became Canada's first incorporated city in 1785.

The citizens of Charlottetown awoke on November 17, 1775, to find two strange vessels entering the harbour, preparing to fire on the town. Philips Callbeck, acting for the absent governor, had no soldiers and could not defend the town. Thinking perhaps the ships contained pirates, who could be paid to go away, Callbeck met the visitors – probably with justified trepidation. One captain, John Selman, ordered Callbeck seized and taken aboard the *Franklin*. The other, Captain Broughton of the *Hancock*, took privateers to Fort Amherst and damaged the cannon so that the British could not fire them.

The American captains and crews went to the government storehouse and town warehouses, stealing or destroying the contents. Callbeck's home and office were ransacked, government documents were read and the Great Silver Seal, given to the colony by the king, was stolen. Privateers searched for Mrs. Callbeck, but fortunately she had fled upriver. The sailors threatened to take her life because she was the daughter of a known supporter of King George III. They smashed their way into the governor's residence, stealing furniture, carpets, curtains, looking glasses, even bedding and the spice cabinet, a treasure in those days.

The privateers sailed away with their prisoners. Reaching Winter Harbour, now in Maine, they forced the prisoners to march 120 miles along the coast to Cambridge, then the headquarters of General George Washington. He was angry with the two captains, who had been ordered not to attack anyone but the British, and ordered the settlers' stolen goods returned, but they had already been sold. Washington gave Callbeck permission to hire a vessel to return home, but winter weather delayed them until the spring of 1776.

"I found Charlottetown to be wicked enough for a far larger place," said an early visitor.

The Great Silver Seal was never recovered. Fortunately, a wax copy had been made, so the images (a crest on one side and a large oak beside three smaller ones on the other) were not lost. Those who fared the worst were 103 settlers who lost most of their winter supplies. They nearly starved to death.

There was more goodwill than animosity between the border towns of St. Stephen, New Brunswick, and Calais, Maine. During the War of 1812, St. Stephen lent gunpowder to Calais for its Fourth of July celebration, and the friendship between the two towns has become legendary.

LUNENBURG OR LÜNEBURG?

England was keen to increase the non-French population in our part of the New World, but not enough willing British settlers could be found. John Dick, hired to bring in Germans (recognized as fine pioneers), received a guinea for each. He managed to round up some 2,400, mostly Germans and Swiss but also some French Protestants who were not especially well treated in Catholic France. They came seeking free land, lower taxes and freedom from a war they felt brewing in Europe. The first arrived in Halifax in 1750, too late to clear land before the snows fell. Over the next few years, their numbers grew, but they were disappointed to be kept working on the forts and building barracks by Governor Cornwallis, who was determined to shore up defenses.

In the spring of 1753, 14 small ships sailed from Halifax, loaded with German, French and Swiss determined to build a town at Lunenburg. With its fine harbour, proximity to Halifax and excellent land, it was considered ideal. By the end of June, the population had swelled to 1,500 or so. Each man was given a town lot, a garden lot and land farther away to clear for farming. Who got what was determined by drawing from a deck of cards. Some of descendants of those first settlers have those cards still today.

Although the people wanted to work at planting gardens and clearing fields, fortifications were the first priority. Some Natives, realizing these newcomers intended to stay, had killed or kidnapped settlers who strayed. Creature comforts were neglected while strong homes, fortifications and a wall around the town were built. The houses of early Lunenburg would seem strange today. Square with walls six feet high made of poles or trees roughly straightened by an axe. Doors and shutters of thick planks bolted with iron, for they had to be very strong to keep out intruders.

Things gradually improved. Land was cleared and crops were harvested, and, more important, farmers learned how to build boats and how to fish. The grandchildren of people who had little experience of the ocean became the finest fishers and sailors in the world. The ocean became the main highway to Halifax. Lunenburgers were industrious and thrifty and quickly became known as having one of the most prosperous towns in the province.

Prior to the arrival of the German settlers, it was decreed that the new settlement would be called Lunenburg as an expression of loyalty to the royal house of Braunschweig-Lüneburg, whose elector became King George I of England in 1714.

Lunenburg has had its seafaring past documented in the Fisheries Museum of the Atlantic – a truly wonderful place to spend a day. Another of Lunenburg's assets is a wealth of 19th-century architecture, which has resulted in its listing as a National Heritage Historic District. A further honour came in 1995 when the town was designated a World Heritage Site by UNESCO.

The first Jewish settlers in the Maritimes were probably the four Hart brothers who settled near the naval base at Halifax in 1751. Jews had been denied entrance to Canada throughout the French regime. In 1793 Samuel Hart was the first Jew to be elected MLA of Nova Scotia, representing Liverpool.

In 1872, 29 Danish immigrants arrived, eager to settle the tracts of land available to them in New Brunswick. A long and arduous journey up the St. John River and then overland through dense woods and rocky ground only to face several years of great hardship did not daunt these pioneers. Today their heritage is evident in the town of New Denmark, particularly in traditional dishes such as herring in sour cream. On Founders Day in June, costumes, folk dances and entertainment celebrate both the season and the culture.

HERITAGE OF ADVERSITY

For almost four centuries, blacks have made the Maritimes their home – some by choice, others against their will. They came from Africa, the West Indies and the United States. Some came as free men and women lured by the promise of free land. Others came as slaves.

As early as 1606, Matthieu de Costa, a former slave of the Portuguese, lived at Port-Royal. Between 1713 and 1760, as many as 175 black servants served French masters at Fort Louisbourg. By 1750 at least a dozen free blacks were living in Halifax. A year later, slaves helped to build a ship there. The 1767 census reported 104 people of African descent among Nova Scotia's population of 13,374.

Things changed dramatically in 1783 when the Loyalists arrived, counting 3,000 blacks among them. This was the first wave of black immigration.

Things did not go well for these immigrants. Although the British had lured Loyalists with promises of land, rations and farming implements, they had not anticipated the response and simply could not fulfill the promises as quickly as they should have. As a result, many Loyalists, particularly blacks, were literally left out in the cold. By the time the government lived up to its promises it was too little too late. In 1792, 1,196 black Loyalists departed Halifax for Sierra Leone.

The second black immigration, in 1796, brought 543 Maroons who had been deported from Jamaica; the third, from 1812 to 1814, saw an estimated 2,000 refugees arrive from Chesapeake in the United States. Between 1899 and 1912, West Indian blacks emigrated to Cape Breton to work in the steel and mining industries.

Despite the early struggles and disappointments, many black immigrants, particularly the refugees, remained. Their descendants people communities such as Hammonds Plains, Tracadie, Sunnyville, Yarmouth, Weymouth Falls, Granville Ferry, Kentville, the Prestons, Sydney, Antigonish and Springhill. Like other ethnic or racial groups, those who were determined survived the adversity.

William Hall, the Nova Scotian son of escaped slaves, was one of the first Canadians to receive the British Empire's highest award for bravery, the Victoria Cross. Hall was part of a troop sent to rescue a small British garrison under siege at Lucknow, India. The key to Lucknow was the Shah Nujjiff, a walled mosque, itself enclosed by yet another wall. The outer wall was breached by Highlanders at midday, and Hall's brigade dragged its guns within 400 metres of the inner wall. The walls were thick, and by late afternoon the 30,000 Sepoy defenders had inflicted heavy casualties. The guns were dragged still closer to the walls. A bayonet attack had little effect. Two guns were ordered to within 20 metres of the wall, drawing a concentration of enemy fire. Only Hall was left able to fire. He continued working his gun until it finally opened the walls. "I remember," Hall is quoted as saying, "that after each round we ran our gun forward, until at last my gun's crew were actually in danger of being hurt by splinters of brick and stone borne by the round shot from the walls we were bombarding."

THE REPUBLIC OF MADAWASKA

After their War of Independence, the Americans were not prepared to give up all they desired. The boundary between New Brunswick and Maine had not been clearly defined. It changed so often that people were not sure in just which country they lived. Tired of being pawns in the skirmishes and tortuous political negotiations, the people, scorning the authorities, decided to "found" the République de Madawaska. Its borders more or less encompassed the area settled by the French-speaking population. The borders, at least as far as the English and Americans were concerned, were finally settled after the Aroostook War, generally known as the Pork and Beans War ('cause that was all they ate?). March 25, 1839, marked a compromise, and later an agreement was reached between Lord Ashburton and the eminent American jurist Daniel Webster.

Although the Republic is not formally independent, the people of the region have long defined themselves as citizens of the Republic of Madawaska and call themselves Brayons. The name might come from the word brayer, meaning "crush," because crushing flax was a common chore for Madawaskan ancestors in France. The Brayons are descendants of both Québécois and Acadians. The former came to New Brunswick in the 18th and 19th centuries seeking new land to settle, whereas the latter were driven from the lower St. John River by an influx of Loyalist colonists at the end of the 18th century.

The republic has its own president – namely, the mayor of Edmundston – and its own coat of arms, which was duly registered in Ottawa in 1949. It also has its own flag, featuring a brown eagle with a white head surrounded by six red stars, which represent the cultural groups that make up the population: Native, Acadian,

Canadian, English, American and Irish.

The skirmishes between New Brunswick and Maine have left a legacy of humorous stories, songs and ongoing traditions. Of the many war songs, the Americans sang this one lustily:

> We'll lick the red-coats anyhow,
> And drive them from our border;
> The loggers are awake – and all
> Await the Gin'ral's order;
> Britannia shall not rule the Maine,
> Nor shall she rule the water;
> They've sung that song full long enough,
> Much longer than they oughter.

The only British prime minister born outside the British Isles was Andrew Bonar Law of Rexton, New Brunswick.

John Baker, a longtime resident, tired of not knowing which country he lived in, decided to publicly cast his vote by flying an American flag in Madawaska. The constable from Woodstock took it down; Baker put up another. Then New Brunswick's governor heard of the hijinks and sent the sheriff, who arrested Baker in his bed. Some say the "flag" was no more than a pair of red bloomers belonging to the rather large girlfriend of Paddy McGarrigle, a cook in a New Brunswick lumber camp. Bloomers or no, Baker was tried and sentenced to three months in jail.

McGarrigle shared a sense of humour as well as a friendship with Baker. Paddy and his girl strolled across the border to Fairfield, Maine. The duo – resplendent in red, he in breeches and a mackinaw, she in a mammoth dress – found the village deserted and "claimed" it for England. Paddy joked that when the residents saw them they thought it was the whole redcoat army and ran away. Truth is that they were probably in church.

When the Webster-Ashburton Treaty ended the arguments in 1842, John Baker found himself still living in New Brunswick.

One of Canada's unsung heroines was Sarah Edmonds of Magaguadavic, New Brunswick. Born in 1849, she had a yearning for adventure that lured her across the border to New England. Realizing that men had far more opportunities than women, she disguised herself as a boy and quickly rose in the hierarchy of bookselling. Her dual roles allowed her to experience life as few women did in her time. As a nurse in the Civil War, she was on the field at Bull Run. As a supposed man using the moniker Franklin Thompson, she joined the U.S. army and served in an infantry division as a spy, mail carrier and soldier. Her ability with disguise allowed her to infiltrate Confederate lines as a black, a clerk, a rebel cavalryman and a boy. Sarah did marry. A Saint John lumberman named Linus Seelye wooed her during one of her stints nursing. They had three children. Sarah applied for a pension with the U.S. army, and it was only then that the army found out she was a woman. Her $12 a month made her the first female pensioner of the U.S. army. Her autobiography, *Nurse and Spy in the Union Army,* tells all.

The colonies that came to be Canada were invaded by Irish-American troops around the time of the U.S. Civil War. Members of an Irish-American organization called the Fenians in the United States sought to free Ireland from British rule, and they thought that getting control of Canada would perhaps give them the power to do it. Raids were planned in Ontario, Quebec and the Maritimes. In the Maritimes, British forces turned back the Fenians, but for the next several years people along the New Brunswick border lived in fear and were always on the alert. The Fenian raids had a major effect on the British North American colonists, reinforcing John A. Macdonald's arguments that a united country would be better able to muster defense. Resentment against the United States government, which did little to hinder the raids, also boosted the drive toward Confederation.

CONFEDERATION:
A MIXED BLESSING

Between 1864 and 1867, a series of meetings was held in Quebec, Halifax, Saint John and Charlottetown. John A. Macdonald, representing what would become Ontario, said, "We must have some form of colonial unity. We seek to found a great land… we must seek it now."

Although Charlottetown is known as the "Cradle of Confederation" the truth is the conference was set up to discuss a Maritime union, not form the country of Canada. Delegates from Canada were invited to attend only in response to a special request from their governor general. The Hon. George Brown, Upper Canadian Reform leader and a senior member of the Canadian delegation, wrote to his beloved wife, Anne, in glowing terms of Island hospitality and of the business at hand.

"When the conference adjourned [for the day], we all proceeded on board our steamer and the members were entertained at luncheon in princely style. [Lower Canada's rep George-Etienne] Cartier and I made eloquent speeches, of course, and whether as the result of our eloquence or of the goodness of our champagne, the ice became completely broken, the tongues of the delegates wagged merrily, and the banns of matrimony between all the Provinces of B.N.A. having been formally proclaimed and all manner of persons duly warned there and then to speak or forever after to hold their tongues, no man appeared to forbid the banns and the union was thereupon formally completed and proclaimed!"

It's kind of cool to think bubbly played a role in the formation of our nation.

New Brunswick in particular had close connections with Maine, both in business and through families but when the Americans intercepted a British ship, the *Trent*, on the high seas, it set off a diplomatic crisis that saw several thousand British regulars dispatched by sled through New Brunswick. The whole operation emphasized the need for a railway and organized defense. Still, New

Brunswick politicians were not keen on the idea of giving up the freedom of action that they had.

Prince Edward Islanders were also not eager to sever links with the United States, recognizing that much of the prosperity experienced prior to Confederation came about through a reciprocity agreement with their southern neighbours. In 1868 a U.S. trade delegation was sent to Charlottetown to renew the agreement but was quickly advised by the Colonial Office that the Island's foreign affairs were handled by London. Slapped down by the Mother Country, the Island decided to go it along, defying Confederation until 1873.

It was a time of political turmoil. The northern colonies were splintered, separated by distance, and a civil war had broken out to the south. The question of defense was on many minds.

Halifax has the oldest naval dockyard in North America, established in 1759.

The struggle for reform was not as bitter in the Maritimes as it was in the old colonies of Upper and Lower Canada, now united as one. Nevertheless, in each colony the real power of controlling the government rested in the hands of a small influential group who worked closely with the governor. With elections, things gradually changed, and those eager for reform led the way in passing laws that they felt people wanted. Patience paid off. When responsible government was finally achieved, it came first to Nova Scotia. Reform had come to the Maritimes without rebellion and bloodshed.

Confederation? That was another matter entirely. The Maritime colonists were evenly divided over whether or not to join. Some say the majority were against it. But federating forces carried the day. Strongly influenced by the British government, and worried about the threat posed by the feisty new nation to the south, Ontario, Quebec, Nova Scotia and New Brunswick, by virtue of the British North America Act, were united, effective July 1, 1867.

Many Nova Scotians complained, bitterly outraged over the loss of their right to free trade with New England. Black arm bands were worn to mourn the economic death of Nova Scotia. For a while, a movement to secede from the new union was afoot. The pro-Confederation party of Charles Tupper in Nova Scotia was slung out of office in elections held later in the year. In fact, Nova Scotia's legislature never officially ratified Confederation.

If the three Maritime Colonies had united in the 1860s, they would have been the fourth-largest shipping nation in the world.

No doubt about it, with Confederation, a new era arrived. The Maritimes had once profited from their location on the sea, but Confederation made them a less significant area at the edge of a much larger territory. Development of the new country's interior became the main goal, spurred by a new mode of transportation, the railway. To encourage manufacturing, a new import tariff was imposed on all the provinces and territories. The Maritimes could no longer trade freely with other ports. The end of free trade and the introduction of the railway meant that the age of sail and Maritime prosperity was over.

Although Prince Edward Island has been memorialized as the Cradle of Confederation, in fact it did not join Canada until 1873. The island got in a huff in 1867. Islanders wanted the capital of Canada to be in Charlottetown. There was also great trepidation of being a tiny fish in a big pond. Representation by population pretty well ensured that the island would have little control over its destiny. Even a last-minute offer to buy island land from absentee landlords for $800,000 did not persuade islanders to join. They decided to "stand off and watch the game for a little while."

Islanders also turned down Confederation at first because a transcontinental railway – one of the major unifying obsessions of the rest of Canada – did not interest them. Instead, they decided to build a railway from one end of the island to the other. Every little town wanted a track, of course, and costs mushroomed; being small and isolated, the island found it difficult to borrow money. By 1873 the railway had run up a huge debt of $3,250,000, or about $35 per person. Compared to a big rise in taxes, Confederation looked pretty darn good. Canada upped the ante. Along with the land purchase, it took over the province's debts, most of them from the railway, and promised a year-round ferry service from the mainland and a telegraph line.

Less than three weeks after the island joined Confederation, on July 1st, the Canadian governor general paid a state visit. Much to-do was made of the event, and the procession passed under a grand archway emblazoned with the words "Long courted, won at last!" The dignitary later told a friend that the islanders seemed to think that it was the dominion that had been annexed to the island.

There was great debate about the name that Confederation would bestow on our new country. Suggestions sent to the Toronto Globe in November 1864 included Tupona, from the first letters of The United Provinces of North America, and British Esfiga, from the first letters of English, Scottish, French, Irish, German and Aboriginal. All in all, I'm glad they settled on Canada!

Our Mother Tongues

One day, while driving in Cape Breton, I realized just how multilingual the Maritimes are. Gaelic, English and French are spoken by portions of our population. Micmac is being preserved by the Native residents. There are pockets of Brayon, a dialect older than our nation. Then there are the many families who preserve the language of their homeland. English and less frequently French provide the common denominators, ensuring that the lines of communication always work.

Cape Breton has a third official language: Micmac. Most of the people speak English, some Acadians speak French, and in five Native communities Micmac is the choice for both the spoken and the written word. The village of Chapel Island-Potloteck has made it the official language for conducting community affairs. It is believed to be the first in Atlantic Canada to make such a declaration. Chapel Island-Potloteck has long been considered the cultural cradle of the Micmac Nation, and the Grand Council meets there twice a year.

It is believed that Micmac hieroglyphics are the oldest form of indigenous writing in North America. Anthropology student David Schmidt of the University of California went to Eskasoni in 1992 because, he says, Micmac is also the only linguistic system in the world that is word based – each symbol represents a word rather than a letter. His visit to gather research for his Ph.D dissertation turned into a year-long stay when he received funding from the Dioceses of Antigonish to print a revised edition of an 1866 Catholic prayer book in its original hieroglyphic form with translations into

New Brunswick is Canada's only officially bilingual province, with 35 percent of the population speaking Acadian French and the rest speaking English.

both Micmac and English. There are more than 5,000 word symbols in hieroglyphics.

It is thought that the symbols were used prior to the arrival of French missionaries. In the 1650s, missionary Chrestien LeClercq reported using the system to teach prayers.

During the 1730s-50s, Abbé Pierre Maillard produced versions of church liturgies to teach Micmacs mass, baptism and sacraments in the belief that he would be the last Catholic priest. His prediction proved true for many years after the fall of New France. Chiefs acted as priests for their communities.

The reprinting of the prayer book was a gift to the community on the 250th anniversary of the first St. Anne's Mission of Chapel Island, arranged by Bishop Colin Campbell. It was published by the University of Cape Breton Press. Schmidt also had a great interest in producing a hieroglyphic dictionary.

Other examples of the use of hieroglyphics are found in the Micmac Legal Codes of 1739 and the 1749 Declaration of War against the British.

Silas Tertius Rand, born in 1810 in Cornwallis, Nova Scotia, joined a Baptist ministry at the age of 24, devoting his life to the Micmac as the first Protestant missionary to the Natives of Nova Scotia. He showed a great gift for languages and compiled a 40,000-

word *Dictionary of the Language of the Micmac Indians* and translated the Bible into the Micmac tongue. One of 22 children, Silas had very little formal schooling.

Gaelic, used for centuries in the Highlands and Islands of Scotland, is still used in some parts of Nova Scotia and appears on road signs. You can learn Gaelic and other Celtic arts at the Gaelic College in Cape Breton. *Caid mile failte* are words commonly seen; Gaelic for "one hundred thousand welcomes," they are pronounced "kaid mee-la falja."

There are several places in the Maritimes where you can experience life as it was in days gone by. Two of the best are Kings Landing Historical Settlement near Fredericton and Fortress Louisbourg in Cape Breton. At Kings Landing, people live so realistically in the past that you want to join them. In fact, under a program called Visiting Cousins, children can spend a week in costume immersed in the life and chores of days past. Traditional meals are served at the inn, with special feasts for special occasions such as Christmas. You must reserve for those!

CHAPTER 2

WHERE
WE LIVE

"I have traveled around the globe, I have seen the Canadian and American Rockies, the Andes and the Alps and the Highlands of Scotland; but for sheer simple beauty, Cape Breton outrivals them all."

– Alexander Graham Bell

Eons ago, the Maritimes were a far different place. New Brunswick was under the sea. Mainland Nova Scotia was covered with tropical forests and was located near the equator. Apparently, it sort of drifted up here and glommed onto the rest of us. Once New Brunswick had risen, and Nova Scotia had become fixed, a piece of the mass gradually separated, becoming what we now know as Prince Edward Island. It's all very complex and happened as many as 300 million years ago.

Let there be no doubt: the Maritimes are astonishing in their diversity. The landscape changes rapidly from region to region. Even the coast ranges from the craggy shores of the Atlantic Ocean to the tidal mud flats and bays of the Bay of Fundy to the sand-washed beaches of the Gulf of St. Lawrence.

As distances go, we are not vast. You can drive through each province in a day, although the amazing variety of terrain and scenery can give the impression of travelling great distances.

The land and the sea are inseparable and together with climatic challenges have dared the peoples who have lived here to adapt to what nature decrees. Settlement began along the coasts and rivers. In the early days, tracks followed the routes of least resistance, skirting waterways, through valleys and around natural obstacles. These tracks became our roads. Although we have a few four-laners, most of the highways still seem to meander. They're part of the charm of the Maritimes.

In the winter, travel used to be difficult. There were no snowblowers or snowploughs to clear the roads, no radio to warn of storms. Communities tended to be isolated for several months a year. People helped one another cope and in the process created the bonds and the community spirit for which the region is known. Even today, with the modern world bringing rapid change, community and neighbours still matter in the Maritimes. Life is a little slower paced, a little more relaxed. Citizens tend to have their priorities right.

Add to the community spirit the wonderful scenery and the easier pace that allows life to be savoured and you have a combination that many visitors have fallen in love with. From the earliest settlements on, this region has lured people wishing for a new start, for a simpler, better life in which values have not gone astray.

An amazing number of Maritimers have arrived here seeking the good life. Many have found it. Many Maritimers, on the other hand, leave, seeking work, education and what they perceive as a better life. Many return home after a few years away. Kind of keeps the balance.

THOSE VERY OLDEN DAYS

The whole of New Brunswick was under the sea when volcanic upheavals, similar to those in Iceland today, pushed it up. Some 370 million years ago, give or take, when the ancient continents of Laurentia and Gondwanaland collided, the province was fused to what are today Eastern Greenland, Scotland and Norway. The Bay of Fundy's coastline still looks like the western part of Scotland.

Cape Breton Island and the mainland are geologically different. Cape Breton is part of an "uplands" – an extension of an old land surface found in parts of New England, the Eastern Townships of Quebec and parts of New Brunswick and Newfoundland.

The Bay of Fundy was formed by "block faulting," the same process that created East Africa's great Rift Valley. Some 320 million years ago, in the early Carboniferous Period, the Earth's crust broke into huge vertical cracks or faults and thus formed giant blocks. Some of the blocks rose. Others, like the Bay of Fundy, fell.

During this period, the Bay of Fundy was hot and dry, with a climate similar to that of California's Death Valley – hard to imagine today, especially on a cool, foggy morning. Some 15 million years later, the weather turned more humid, and the Appalachian Rift Valley, of which New Brunswick was a part, became covered with swamps and mangrove forests, similar to those found at the mouth of the Amazon and Ganges Rivers today.

Clues to the past can be found all around the Bay of Fundy. The sandstone cliffs and sea coves to the east of St. Martins, sculpted into dramatic headlands by the tides, are reminiscent of the flat-topped mesas of Arizona — not surprising, because the rocks belong to the same period.

Shades of Jurassic Park… The towering red sea cliffs of Joggins on Chignecto Bay and Wassons Bluff on Minas Basin lure people from around the world to see the dinosaur fossils. In 1986 the biggest fossil find in North America from the late Triassic and early Jurassic Periods – the time when dinosaurs were first emerging as the dominant land animal – occurred. This find helped to establish the Bay of Fundy's reputation as one of the classic fossil locations in the Western Hemisphere. From one block of earth, 100,000 fossilized bones belonging to ancient crocodiles, lizards, sharks, fish and of course dinosaurs were found. Among this treasure were the oldest dinosaurs – some by 70 million years – ever found in Canada.

Mastodons are known to have roamed near the Bras d'Or Lakes 30,000 years ago. A mastodon thighbone found near Middle River, Cape Breton, in 1835 has been radio-carbon dated at about 30,000 years. It is now on display at the Nova Scotia Museum of Natural History in Halifax. In 1983 an archaeologist noticed unusual little gouges in the bone. They might have been caused by natural weathering or made by stone tools during butchering. If they are butchering marks, then people hunted here 30,000 years ago, 20,000 years earlier than other evidence has shown. Only redating the bone and further research will provide the answer.

And there's more. In October 1991, one of the most exciting paleontological discoveries in Nova Scotia occurred when a heavy equipment operator at the National Gypsum Quarry in Milford unearthed a tusk and some large teeth. They were identified as being from a mastodon, and the museum folks immediately began a full-scale recovery. The mastodon was situated halfway up the exposed mud wall of a partially excavated sinkhole. About 12 to 15 tonnes of earth were removed from the site, along with the bones. Everything found was carefully cleaned, preserved and catalogued. It is thought that the animal was part of a herd, because a juvenile mastodon was also found at the site, along with traces of plants and other animals. The bones are believed to be 79,000 years old, from a male mastodon about 22 years of age that died in the spring. Mastodons were equal in size to the largest African elephants and had huge tusks. A replica of this mastodon stands high on Mastodon Ridge at Stewiacke seeming to trumpet his displeasure at traffic passing on the nearby Trans-Canada Highway.

FiNDiNG YOUR BEARiNGS

One of the best ways to get an appreciation for the Maritime provinces and their diverse regions is to study a map. You will see that Nova Scotia, vaguely shaped like a lobster, missed being an island because of the Isthmus of Chignecto, which at its narrowest is only 27 kilometres (17 miles) across. New Brunswick is a solid block of land, looking strong and immovable – the anchor. Prince Edward Island lies offshore, cradled by its larger cousins but distinct – an entity on its own.

N ova Scotia is virtually a peninsula, with the Gulf of St. Lawrence to the north, the Bay of Fundy to the west and the Atlantic Ocean to the south and east. The province divides into many areas. I offer four to show the diverse geography: the rugged granite of the Atlantic Coast, with large bays and islands; Fundy's Annapolis Valley, with soil described as Devonian or Red African, which supports lush orchards, vineyards and horse farms; Northumberland Shore, with endless beaches backed by heavily forested hills; and Cape Breton Island, where the Cabot Trail takes you through a land of fjords, mountains, cliffs and stunning vistas.

Bras d'Or Lake on Cape Breton is the world's largest saltwater lake.

P rince Edward Island, a smiling, crescent shape, is surrounded by Northumberland Strait on the south shore and the Gulf of St. Lawrence on the north shore. The coast is rimmed with spectacular sand dunes, sculpted sandstone cliffs, saltwater marshes and both white and red sand beaches. Rolling hills and rich red earth dominate the province's landscape. Its irregular shape, with bays and inlets galore, means that you are never far from saltwater. Summer visitors marvel at the multitude of greens, the patchwork of fields, woodlands against the blue of sea and sky.

Some folks, looking at Prince Edward Island's patchwork of fields and farms, might notice that they appear, well, slanted. As you drive toward the north shore, you are invariably drawn northwest, and property boundaries are noticeably set out in regimented rows imposed parallel or perpendicular to each other. The lay of the land rarely had any bearing on this division. Imaginary lines seem to slice through estuaries and bays.

No point in Nova Scotia is more than 56 kilometres from the sea.

It was the British who did it. Well practised in surveying and cartography by the mid-1700s, they decided to assess their freshly conquered territories. Captain Samuel Holland was appointed surveyor general of much of North America, and he set to work dividing the island into three counties, approximately 20,000 acres each, with the "greatest precision and exactness" that did not waver even over the shifting sand dunes and rolling valleys. The Micmac must have thought the survey teams daft as they penetrated the deep woods using dogsleds and canoes rather than take the river.

Captain Holland and his crew of apprenticing assistants, Acadian guides and British redcoats surveyed by taking magnetic north as the cardinal direction, making a deflection of 15 degrees off today's true north and influencing us now and always to "north by northwest."

New Brunswick, almost rectangular in shape, extends about 322 kilometres from north to south and 242 kilometres from east to west. It is bordered by water on most of two sides. Mountainous terrain is predominant in the northern part of the province; the interior is mostly rolling plateau, the eastern portion is fairly flat and the southern part is rugged.

The "brownstones" used to build townhouses in Boston and New York in the 1800s came from quarries around the inner part of the Bay of Fundy. The sandstone outcrops around Cape Enrage, Mary's Point, Grindstone Island and Dorchester were formed during the late Carboniferous Period. The stone is grey when cut, but because of its high iron content it weathers to the colour of rust.

NATURE'S BOUNTY:
·ON LAND & SEA

The Maritimes are home to an abundant diversity of plants and animals, with an astonishing range of species for such a small region. Nova Scotia claims to be home to more rare plants and animals than any other area of comparable size in North America.

Things official:

	Nova Scotia	Prince Edward Island	New Brunswick
Flower	Mayflower	Lady's Slipper	Purple Violet
Bird	Osprey	Blue Jay	Chickadee
Tree	Red Spruce	Red Oak	Balsam Fir

Prince Edward Islanders don't pay much attention to Groundhog Day because they don't have any groundhogs! Didn't have any skunks either until some bright spark decided to import them for a fur-breeding business. It failed. He turned the skunks loose, and

Prince Edward Island has 1,760 kilometres of coastline.

Islanders have been cursing ever since. Skunks have few predators and multiply so fast it's sinful. In fact their main enemy is the automobile. Hundreds of skunks bite the pavement as soon as the sun begins to warm the earth in late winter, luring them from their holes. Generally, it all creates a great stink and makes leaving the dog out a risky business.

It's for the birds! There are more than 275 known species of birds in the Maritimes. At least, that's what's left after a few centuries of human contact. About 100 years ago, feathered hats were considered stylish. Tern feathers, even entire birds, decorated women's hats. The slaughter almost wiped out colonies along the eastern coast of North America. Sable Island terns were protected both by distance and an 1801 rule prohibiting access to the island without permission from the island's commissioner. When the International Migratory Bird Convention Act of 1916 protected terns, coastal colonies quickly recovered, probably restocked with birds from Sable Island.

 In 1980 New Brunswick's Furbish lousewort became the first plant to be protected under the Endangered Species Act.

A wild-bird sanctuary located at Mary's Point, down Highway 915 from the village of Alma (located at the entrance to Fundy National Park), sees hundreds of thousands of semipalmated sandpipers alight between mid-July and mid-August each year.

Sable Island and its inhabitants are probably the most studied aspects of nature in the region. The isolation makes Sable Island a great laboratory.

When plants or animals breed in isolation, they often develop unique characteristics and can evolve into new species. Sable Island grass-pink orchid leaves, for example, are more oblong than those on parents on the mainland.

Ducks probably brought their own dinner to Sable Island. Tiny freshwater pea clams may have hitchhiked to the island by clamping on to ducks for a free flight. Because pea clams can reproduce from a single individual, it is also possible that the entire population came from one clam.

Every year the Gulf Stream carries eel larvae to Sable Island. Storm waves wash them over into Lake Wallace, where the fresh water triggers their slow change into adults. During rainy weather, eels slither overland into the island's freshwater ponds.

Tropical beans are often found on the beaches after floating up from the Caribbean. They don't germinate. It's too cold.

Two kinds of insects and a freshwater sponge are found only on Sable Island. Some biologists think they survived the Ice Age.

Walrus bred on Sable Island from the Ice Age to the 1600s. Hunted for oil and ivory, they were driven to extinction. In 1642, 400 tusks were taken.

The largest bald eagle population east of the Rockies calls Nova Scotia home.

Oysters near the island became extinct at least 5,000 years ago, and bay scallops disappeared 2,000 years ago.

Deep-sea corals are usually associated with colourful reefs in the tropics. However, they also live in the cold waters of northern seas. Living deep in the sea, they never experience sunlight. They feed by catching small animals on outstretched tentacles. There are two main groups: stony corals and flexible horny corals. Fishers in Nova Scotia have given local corals descriptive names, such as bubble gum tree, mushroom coral, birch trees, sea corn and black coral.

Lobsters moult… just like dogs and cats. Difference is, they are a little neater about it, shedding the whole shell at once instead of dropping tufts of hair in the wake of the vacuum cleaner. The crustacean basically splits its old shell, crawls out and leaves it behind. Although a new shell has started growing, it is soft, and the lobster is very vulnerable – cod and other aggressors are eager to enjoy a lobster supper.

The lobster quickly finds a good hiding place in the mud or among the rocks, puffs up a couple of sizes and waits for the new, bigger shell to harden. Once the process is complete, the excess water used to puff up the body is released, and our lobster has growing room for another year.

The exception occurs when a female decides she wants to be a mom. As soon as she has shed her shell, she heads out to lure a fellow out of his hole, throws herself on her back and begins mating. The two then usually shack up together for a while. Once her new shell is in place, though, Mom tends to wander off.

The shell that remains after a lobster discards it gives testimony to the miracle. Only a split down the back shows where the former tenant exited. Think about this. The big claws are slipped through the knuckles and leg joints – a space about one-fifth their size!

A new life form was found on the *Titanic* when undersea explorers visited the famous wreck in their submersible. Rusticles, icicle-like forms draped on the metal frame of the downed liner, are microbiologically complex structures that can reach lengths greater than one metre.

THE BAY OF FUNDY

One of the things on my wish list is the time to indulge in a scenic coastal tour of the Bay of Fundy, preferably on a motorcycle so that I can truly enjoy the scents, the sounds, the air and, of course, the scenic wonders. My trip would take in every little fishing village, every lighthouse and every campground as I sweep up the Nova Scotia side to the east and down the western New Brunswick side. To do it properly, I'd need two weeks.

The tides of the Bay of Fundy are one of the most incredible natural phenomena on Earth. Twice a day, nature puts on a show when the tides, the highest in the world, rush in at an amazing rate. The funnel-like bay causes the water to rise as much as 23 metres (think of a five-storey building) in just six and a half hours, a flow equal to all the water in all the rivers in the world.

The landscape of the coast is changed. Fishing boats that bobbed merrily beside a wharf at high tide end up tilted over, lying on their keels on the mud, when the water recedes. Tidal rivers and streams become mini clay gorges, with sides so slick that little grows on them.

The Bay of Fundy has a personality all its own, dominating the landscape and dictating its own terms to those who live by the sea. Incoming tides are so strong that they actually reverse the flow of a waterfall and create a tidal bore (small tidal wave) in the Petitcodiac River. The Reversing Falls of Saint John, another wonder, are caused by the tides rushing through a rocky gorge into the St. John River – all in the old part of town, so it's nice and convenient for the curious.

The Petitcodiac River is known locally as the Chocolate River because of its colour.

One of the more famous individuals to be enamoured of the Fundy islands was the artist and scientist James Audubon. In the early 19th century, he was drawn by the 275 or so species of birds that land on Grand Manan Island each year and by the magnificent rock formations and scenery. A mecca for nature lovers, with excellent trails running along the shoreline, Grand Manan is a point of departure for whale-watching excursions and for expeditions to Machias Seal Island, with its wonderful bird sanctuary.

Is it whales you want? The Bay of Fundy boasts an ocean galaxy of 15 or so kinds of whales drawn by the rich feeding grounds. It is one of the world's most accessible sites for viewing marine mammals. Experts say the high tides stir up nutrient-rich water up to the surface twice a day causing immense blooms of plankton – sort of like offering free burgers and fries to teenagers!

Most whales are sighted infrequently, but four are commonly seen:

- Finback Whales are the giants, the second largest whale in the world, growing up to 24 metres (83 feet) and weigh 73 tonnes (80 tons). Finbacks are a favourite with whale-watchers because they have a tall "blow".

- Right Whales, are one of the world's rarest, and most endangered. There are fewer than 350 of these giants left in the world and they are known to mate in Fundy. Rights are easily identified by their complete lack of a dorsal fin and the bumpy whitish skin patches on their heads.

- Minke Whales are one of the smallest of baleen whales (toothless dudes who have a food-filtering maw). Their sharply pointed snout is often the first thing out of the water unlike most whales whose back breaks first.

- Humpback Whales, often called "clowns of the sea," love to play – which means they are great for photographing as they leap and cavort in the water. They are distinguished by "bumps" of flesh on their snouts and the leading edge of their flippers.

The world-famous "Balancing Rock," a spectacular columnar basaltic sea stack, is found at the shore on Long Island near Tiverton, Nova Scotia. A hiking trail takes you there. Also a great place to catch a whale-watching tour.

St. Martins, a lovely fishing village in New Brunswick, has two covered bridges, one leading to the famous echo caves at Quaco. These tide-scoured cavities are great places to explore at low tide. At the base of the cliffs, brightly coloured stones cover the beach. Just out from the Quaco lighthouse, you can see Dulse Island, where pickers harvest seaweed at low tide. St. Martins prospered during the era of shipbuilding, with as many as 126 vessels under construction at a time during the age of sail.

Old Sow, the world's second largest tidal whirlpool, off Deer Island Point, was so named because it is said to sigh and snort like an old pig. Three hours before high tide, folks on Deer Island can stand on the southernmost point and view Old Sow. Take it from me, it's better viewed this way than from a boat!

Tides have a great influence on our rivers and marshes. The Acadians realized this and reclaimed some of the rich flatlands near shores by building an aboiteau – a dam fitted with a gate that releases fresh water but prevents seawater from flooding through when the tide comes in. These dams were particularly used on the Tantramar Marsh near Sackville, New Brunswick, and at Grand Pré, Nova Scotia, site of the expulsion of the Acadians.

Elephant Rock, sculpted from the sandstone cliffs by nature, lures sightseers to the western tip of Prince Edward Island. A good onshore wind makes for interesting pictures as the sea breaks over the elephant's trunk and front legs.

How's The Weather?

The weather is our greatest topic of conversation, and, when family and friends "away" hear about one of our storms, they make many telephone calls to ensure that loved ones have survived the latest weather event. Hurricanes from the Caribbean, snow from the American Midwest, cold spells from Quebec and Ontario – heck, even El Niño from the Pacific Ocean – they all seem to track to the Maritimes. Following is some information from Environment Canada.

There are a few truisms about Maritime weather:

It can change fast.

It is hard to predict.

For every awful day, there are many more great ones.

> *Nineteen different kinds of sharks are found in our cool waters.*

Prince Edward Island has some of the most variable day-to-day weather experienced anywhere in the country. The island is affected by a mishmash of weather systems, bringing polar, maritime, continental and tropical air from the Arctic, Pacific and Atlantic Oceans and from the Gulf of Mexico. In summer the island is visited most often by continental air from the west. Occasionally, warm tropical air is drawn in from the south. Winters are dominated by cold continental air masses, but storms originating in the North Pacific or the Gulf of Mexico frequently pass through, making winters stormy and unpredictable. The influence of moist Atlantic air often produces warm periods during the winter and cool weather during the summer.

The north shore is said to be warm because the Gulf Stream, a warm water current flowing northward from the tropics, flows into the Gulf of St. Lawrence. Beaches at Shediac and along the Northumberland Strait offer warm waters because the water is shallow for great distances from the shore and quickly warmed by the sun. When the tide is out, the sand warms and transfers the heat to the water as it flows back in.

Perhaps the most significant feature of a New Brunswick winter is the marked variability in temperature from day to day. This is a product of the highly contrasting and fast-moving weather systems which traverse the province every two or three days. New Brunswick has some of the sunniest places in Atlantic Canada: Chatham is the only station in the region to record an average of 2000 hours a year. Surprisingly Saint John is the sunniest spot in eastern Canada in December with an average of 100 hours. In July it has one of the lowest sunshine totals in Canada. Go figure.

The well-mixed Atlantic waters off the Bay of Fundy are among the foggiest areas of the world, although not as notoriously foggy as the Grand Banks of Newfoundland. There is a Mariner's Tale that says, "Sometimes out on the Bay of Fundy when the fog comes in thick you can sit on the boat's rail and lean your back up against it. So that's pretty thick fog out there; but you gotta be careful 'cause if the fog lifts quick you'll fall overboard."

Nova Scotia owes much to the sea, especially its climate. Robust winters, reluctant springs, fresh summers, and lingering falls. Reliable precipitation and lavish snowfalls, misty sunlight, thick fog and expansive sea ice – all of these, and many more are a part of Nova Scotia's maritime climate.

Halifax's reputation as a foggy and misty city is well deserved. Each year there is an average of 122 days with fog at the Halifax International Airport, on the Dartmouth side of the harbour. Not that far away, as the crow flies, southern Nova Scotia claims milder winters than parts of New England and Canada's second mildest winter after that of southern British Columbia. The downside to the mildness can be fog, freezing rain and a damper climate.

Remembered in weather chronicles as the Great Nova Scotia Cyclone, a calamitous hurricane swept over Cape Breton Island on August 25th, 1873. The storm was unusual in having traveled so far to the east after leaving the tropics. Its destructive power was also extraordinary. Ravages of the storm included 1,200 vessels, 500 lives, 900 buildings, and an untold number of bridges, wharve, and dykes. Property losses were conservatively estimated at $3.5 million, an amount equivalent to $70 million in 1990. At the height of the storm, gale-force winds, an intense thunderstorm and heavy rainfalls of 50 mm or more were reported at Halifax, Sydney, and Truro. The Sydney weather observer remarked that this was the worst gale since 1810.

Losses were high, partly because the interruption of telegraph service between Toronto and Halifax prevented storm warnings from getting through. Of significance to Canadian meteorology, this storm, perhaps more than any other event, convinced officials of the need for an improved Canadian storm warning system.

Coping, Maritime style: During the 1998 ice crisis in Ontario and Quebec, which threw thousands of people into turmoil for weeks due to lack of electricity, I was often asked how Maritimers have coped with atrocious weather. You might say that practice makes perfect. Because we have suffered at the hands of the weather, we have learned how to live with its consequences.

Grand Manan Island has been called the Bermuda of the Maritimes because of its benign climate.

For starters, being "storm-stayed" is an acceptable reason for not being somewhere. Storm-stayed means two things. One, you are at home because the roads are impassable. Two, you are away from home when the weather changes and have the good sense to stay put until it improves.

Dealing with power outages is a little easier when you are prepared. When my husband, Jack, and I lived in rural Prince Edward Island, we could be without power for several days. Our worst storm saw the power out for a week. Winds were so furious they took our furnace chimney and the front door. It was bitterly cold, and the snow on the side of the house piled up over the top of the door. Drifts at the end of our drive were so high they were up to the wires on the telephone poles. Once the storm ended, it took four days for huge snowblowers to get in and open the road past our house; then we had to wait for a neighbour to blow out the drive. The drift between the house and the barn was up to the second-storey windows of the house. We had to lug water up and over this drift twice a day to the barn because the pipes froze. We couldn't dig a pathway because the drifting snow filled it in within a couple of hours. It was an adventure we will long remember.

Native orchids are found in all three Maritime provinces.

~~~

HOME BY THE SEA

"I tried to quit the sea, what was there for an old sailor to do? I was born on the breezes and I have studied the sea as perhaps few men have studied it, neglecting all else."
– Joshua Slocum,
the first person to circumnavigate the globe single-handedly by boat,
1895

Joshua Slocum grew up in Westport, Brier Island, Nova Scotia, leaving home at 16 to sail on ocean-going square-riggers. Rising to captain, he survived shipwrecks, mutinies and sickness until the arrival of the steamship deprived him of a sailing command. Joshua set to work and completely rebuilt the hull of an old oyster boat to create the *Spray*. It was a large vessel for one man and possessed a legendary ability to hold a course, aided by a homemade self-steering mechanism. During his voyage, he converted it from a sloop to a yawl by adding a second mast of Nova Scotia spruce.

On December 25, 1897, he rounded the Cape of Good Hope in the *Spray:* "I have to record that while I was at the end of the bowsprit reefing the jib, she ducked me under the water three times for Christmas."

His solo voyage and his account of it, *Sailing Alone around the World,* brought him fame. Even today the book is considered a masterpiece in narrative prose, an enthralling read about life at sea. Published in 1899, it is still in print. Never comfortable on land, Slocum continued to live and roam on the *Spray* until 1905, when – at the age of 65 – he embarked on another voyage and was never heard from again.

Tall ships are often present in our ports. One of the most spectacular tall-ship events in recent history was a fleet that sailed from St-Malo, France, to arrive in Halifax on June 9, 1984, to celebrate the 450th anniversary of Jacques Cartier's voyages.

William Crowell left Halifax on July 16, 1936, in the ketch *Queen Mary*, accompanied by his dog Togo. They reached Vancouver on September 22, 1937, via the Panama Canal after travelling 9,200 miles in 14 months. *Queen Mary* was so small that at one time it was carried on the schooner *Bluenose*, lashed to the deck like a dory.

The "gundalo" or "gundalow," a version of the gondola, is a boat apparently unique to the Maritimes. Its origins are obscure, but four were advertised for sale in a Halifax newspaper in 1753. A general-purpose boat built to carry heavy or bulky cargo, they were mentioned to have carried "sea manure" (eel grass) in Lunenburg in 1819. A photo shows James Bellefontaine hauling marsh hay in 1933, loaded so high it obscured the boat. The boatman could stand on a raised afterplatform to see over the cargo. The boat could be poled, sculled with a sweep or even sailed in a good wind.

Harbour pilots can get "carried away" when adverse weather conditions prevent them from being put off the ship after clearing the harbour. The pilot would then accompany the ship to the port of call. It happened to Halifax harbour pilot Mont Power on the *Aquitania* in the 1940s, taking him to New York. He was presented with a tea service for his trouble.

45

Places We Live

The village of Saint-Joseph-de-Memramcook is important to the Acadians. It is in the only region on the Bay of Fundy where Acadians still live on farmlands occupied before the expulsion. Collège St. Joseph played a key role in keeping Acadian culture alive and well. It was there that Acadian elite were educated for many years. A museum containing artifacts dating back to 1604 was established by Père Camille Lefebvre in 1886 (it was moved to the University of Moncton in 1965).

Greater Halifax, incorporating Halifax, Dartmouth, Bedford and Sackville, with a population of more than 360,000, is on the same latitude as Bordeaux, France, and Portland, Oregon. Its area is 5,577 square kilometres.

Partridge Island, accessible from the port of St. John, was the main point of entry for early immigrants to Canada from the British Isles and Europe. Between 1785 and 1942, it was the transition point and quarantine station for some 3 million immigrants, many of whom settled in the region. About 2,000 had an unhappy end to the arduous voyage across the ocean: they died and were buried on the island.

Amherst, Nova Scotia, is at the geographic centre of the Maritimes.

St. Martins, New Brunswick, is known as the village of sea captains because of the number of square-rigged ships built there in windjammer days – records show at least 390. As happened so often in the Maritimes, many shipbuilders were family businesses. Once the ships were completed, they would be sailed away to be sold, frequently piloted by the builder or a son. The women would anxiously await the return of their menfolk, checking from rooftop platforms called "widows' walks" in the hope of spotting sails returning to port. From Prince Edward Island and likely other ports, these ships were often loaded with lumber that was sold before the vessel itself.

Caught without the foggiest: Everyone who visits magical places such as St. Andrews, New Brunswick, heads home with tales to share. Ours is a fun one. Jack and I went camping just outside St. Andrews at a campground located beside the water. Our friends are not the early risers that we are, so early one summer morning we decided to take a walk before starting breakfast. It seemed logical to give our Welsh corgies a good run on the beach while we waited for our friends to awake.

We strolled out on the tidal flats for quite a distance; then a strange construction of poles and nets loomed up from the fog that had slowly rolled in. It was a fishing weir, and, judging by the height of the nets, we were standing in a place where the water would soon be several feet over our heads. We checked out the weir, resisting the urge to acquire fresh fish for breakfast. Turning to head back to camp, we realized we didn't have the foggiest idea which direction to go. No surf, no traffic, just the occasional cry of a seagull. Once the panic subsided, we thought we could wait for the tide to appear and then just walk ahead of the water until we hit shore. Not the most reassuring idea.

As we unsuccessfully tried to follow our footsteps in the sand, inspiration struck. The dogs. Whistling them in, Jack said, "Come on girls, let's go get breakfast." Duchess and Muggins tilted their heads, looked at each other and trotted away. We did some puffing keeping up with their little legs, but we made it to shore. The fog became so thick we even had trouble finding our campsite. But by the time breakfast was done the summer sun had burned off the mist, and we were all ready for a day of exploring – even the slug-a-beds.

Playground of the rich and famous: Some of the most magnificent structures in the Maritimes began as summer homes for the wealthy from "Upper Canada" and the northeastern United States. Our country inn and bed and breakfast industry, not to mention our museums and historic sites, would not be nearly as interesting without these magnificent structures.

St. Andrews has long attracted the summer resident and has a legacy of magnificent homes to prove it. Among the noteworthy summer residents were:

- Sir Leonard Tilley, one of the Fathers of Confederation
- Sir William Van Horne, chairman of Canadian Pacific Railway, who pushed the rails all the way through the Rocky Mountains
- Lord Thomas Shaughnessy, a financial genius who came from Milwaukee to help complete the railway and succeeded Sir William as CPR chairman
- Lady Beaverbrook, wife of the Canadian-born press baron born Max Aitken, kept a gracious, secluded home called Dayspring near the Algonquin Hotel.
- Tara Manor, the summer home of the late C. D. Howe, is now an inn and restaurant.
- The family of John Turner, former Liberal prime minister, had a family mansion.
- The Hiram Walker Estate Heritage Inn was designed by renowned architect Albert Kahn as a summer home for Edward Chandler Walker, scion of the Hiram Walker Distillery fortune in 1912.

It is said that a small drugstore on Water Street once carried the world's great newspapers for the benefit of the eminent inhabitants of St. Andrews. A powerful clique of financiers and politicians used to gather there to read the papers, drink coffee and discuss the world issues in which they were involved. It's possible that they hatched many schemes affecting the United States, Canada and Britain on this sleepy corner as the sun burned off the salty morning mist.

"Covenhoven," the home of Sir William Van Horne and his wife was actually on Ministers Island, accessible by land only at low tide. It has many unique features, including a swimming pool blasted right out of the rock of the island. Mrs. Van Horne was quite a character, certainly no shy lily. Her husband being a railway builder, she rode the trains a lot, seated on the cowcatcher of the train as it crossed Canada. She would strike up conversations at every stop and knitted to while away the travelling hours. The estate and 50-room mansion can be visited by car at low tide.

Another grand home, not far away as the crow flies, is on Campobello Island. History buffs will tingle with pleasure when stepping onto the island, an impressive example of cooperation between Canada and the United States. The Canadian island is most easily reached from the border town of Lubec, Maine, though a privately run ferry does connect with Deer Island during the summer. Here Campobello International Park, founded in 1964, opens the door to the life of Franklin D. Roosevelt, former American president, and to his magnificent summer home. Roosevelt House vies with the scenic outdoors for your attention.

Canada's oldest French and English wood houses, built in 1708 and 1712 respectively, are in Annapolis Royal, Nova Scotia.

The Pansy Patch, built by well-known Canadian interior decorator and philanthropist Kate Reed, is famous for its unusual architecture. Built in 1912 in French Normandy farmhouse style, it is said to have been fashioned after Jacques Cartier's home in St-Malo, France. In 1994 the St. Andrews home was designated a Canadian Heritage Property. It is considered the most photographed home in New Brunswick.

WHAT DID YA SAY?

Even though we do speak the queen's good English in the Maritimes, you might need a translator from time to time.

"Bluenose" is a nickname applied to Nova Scotians and New Brunswickers. Nineteenth-century humourist Thomas Chandler Haliburton once explained that Canadian shipowners operated a vast number of Maritime-built vessels. Sailing home from the West Indies, loaded with sugar and rum, the captains battled bitterly cold nor'west winds. They took what comfort they could from the rum, which, combined with the winds, turned their noses blue. Hence, they were called the "Bluenose skillers" or simply the "Bluenosers." The explanations of the name put forth by the Nova Scotia government are the large exports of Irish bluenose potatoes to the Carolinas and the blue dye rubbed off the sweaters of fishermen (we needn't ask how it got on their noses).

As early as 1899, a Yarmouth telegram read, in part, "I am down among the 'Herring Chokers' and 'Bluenosers' for a few weeks." Most of us Maritimers think of Bluenosers as being those east of the Bay of Fundy and Herring Chokers as those to the west. In fact, there is an old line: "You know what separates a Bluenoser from a Herring Choker? The Bay of Fundy."

A "time" is a party or special gathering for a celebration. If you are invited to someone's for "dinner," you'd better ask him or her to specify the time on the clock. Dinner is another word for noon lunch, and "supper" is eaten about six p.m. An evening snack is called "bed lunch."

You may hear a comment on the size of the "greybacks," but don't mark yourself as a tourist by looking for whales. Greybacks are the waves washing on the shore.

THE NAMING GAME

Any map of the Maritimes will reveal a mix of names spawned by the languages of early inhabitants. A pride in places of origin, probably mixed with a large measure of homesickness, influenced settlers to give old-country names to villages and towns, rivers and bays. So too did a desire to recognize politicians, great families, achievers and loved ones. Whether family, sponsor or royalty, their names would live on even if memory of them faded.

Prince Charles, when making a speech in Saint John during a royal tour, said how pleased he was to be in St. John's. A collective groan went up from the crowd. "What?" exclaimed the prince. "What did I say wrong?" What had upset his audience was the 's' tacked on to the name Saint John. It is taboo. St. John's is in Newfoundland. One should also always write the Saint out in full. Saint Johners have a right to be proud, for theirs is one of the oldest

European-settled communities in North America; it was incorporated as a city in 1785, 47 years before Quebec City and Montreal and 49 years before Toronto.

The region has some of the most descriptive names in the country, such as rock formations on Grand Manan Island: The Thoroughfare, Head, Whistle Rock, Seven Days Work (seven layers of rock), Hole-in-the-Wall and Swallowtail Light.

In pre-Loyalist days, the open spaces left by cutting the king's pine trees for the Royal Navy were called king's clearings – thus the name of Kingsclear, New Brunswick.

Greenwich, Nova Scotia, located just west of Wolfville, was originally known as Noggins Corner, taking its name from a store that became well known for the sale of "noggins," or wooden mugs, of rum. It seems that some merry times were had at the shop, but the drinking came to an end when one fellow who had overimbibed was killed when he fell from his horse. That event, combined with the growing strength of the temperance movement, was enough to bring about a name change.

In Prince Edward Island, the name Harmony was selected for a school district in Prince County because "the settlers got along peacefully, though of many nationalities: French, Irish, Highland Scottish, Lowland Scottish, English and Dutch." The folks in Kings County, not to be outdone, called a railway stop Harmony Junction, taking the name from New Harmony Road, where, it is said, the various nationalities "also dwelt in harmony." The name was also suggested as a new name for Cornwall when it and surrounding communities amalgamated in 1994. It didn't win.

The French word tintamarre, meaning "hubbub" or "racket," describes the honking of thousands of wild geese and ducks heard by pioneers in what is now known as Tantramar Marsh. Great place for birders.

Originally known as Le Coude ("The Elbow" – of Petitcodiac River), Terre Rouge ("Red Earth" – of the river) or La Chapelle ("The Chapel" – in a rough-hewn log cabin), it became The Bend when Pennsylvania Dutch-German and New England settlers arrived. Today we know it as Moncton, named for Robert Monckton (1726-83), commander of the English expedition against Fort Beauséjour in 1755, later wounded at the Battle of the Plains of Abraham in 1759. A clerical oversight in 1786 caused the 'k' to be dropped. Moncton has been nicknamed the Hub of the Maritimes for its central location. Some say that its geographic centre would make Moncton the ideal capital should the Maritime provinces ever amalgamate.

Pictou was settled in 1767 by immigrants from Philadelphia. The *Hector* in 1773 brought Scottish settlers. The town, built on the site of an ancient Native village, was first called Coleraine, then New Paisley, then Alexandria, then Donegal, followed by Teignmouth (which was too hard to say). Next came Southampton (too English), and then came Walmsley. It is joked that children would wake up and ask, "What is the name of this place today?" In 1790 Pictou (in Micmac, piktook, meaning "explosion" or "fire") was adopted and a solemn resolution made that not another change would be made.

Baie des Chaleurs (Restigouche and Gloucester, New Brunswick) was named by Jacques Cartier during his first voyage to the New World, in early July 1534. He explored the bay and the surrounding territory, which he described as being "more temperate than Spain." Cartier rhapsodized about "wild wheat, as well as pease, as thick as if they had been sown and hoed; white and red currant bushes, straw-berries, raspberries, white and red roses and other plants of a strong, pleasant odour. Likewise," he said, "there are many fine meadows with useful herbs, and a pond where there are many salmon. We named this bay Chaleur Bay (the 'Bay of Heat,' 10 July 1534)." Over the years, the bay has been noted for numerous sightings of a phantom ship, an artistic rendition of which has been incorporated in the logo for the Baie des Chaleurs region tourist authority.

The name of Baie Verte, New Brunswick, near the Nova Scotia border, was inspired by the saltwater grasses that in summer give the bay the appearance of a great meadow. In 1832 Thomas Baillie, the provincial surveyor-general, noted: "Bay Vert gets its name from the quantity of salt water grass which grows in the mud and floats on the surface. It appeared on maps as early as 1701."

Seacow Head, Lot 26 on Prince Edward Island, is derived from the Micmac words bastogobajit waakade, meaning "seacow point." Old documents report that Natives said the point looks like a seacow bent downward. Seacows, or walrus, were once numerous but have long since disappeared. Seacow Pond also gives testimony to the former abundance of these great mammals. In 1847 Abraham Gesner wrote that the area was "the resort of great numbers of the walrus or sea-cow: hundreds of these animals were killed on the land by the early inhabitants, among whose descendants pieces of their skins still remain in use. A deep pond near Tignish is said to be filled with their bones, and their tusks of ivory are occasionally found on the shore, or in the forests. Only a few of those noble animals are now seen, and of their number, which is stated by the fishermen to be on the increase, none are captured." Today the names of these places stand as mute testimony to the importance of preserving our wildlife – for there is nary a seacow to be seen.

Bible Hill, Nova Scotia, received its name in 1761 after its founder, Matthew Archibald, discovered a Bible on a hillside while searching for a pure water spring.

Sometimes both French and English claimed a name as their own. Belfast, Prince Edward Island, according to some, was named by Captain James Smith of HMS *Mermaid* about 1770 for Belfast, Ireland. Not so, say others, it was French for belle face or for a "bell" found "fast" in a swamp.

The St. Lawrence River got its name early. On August 10, 1534, Jacques Cartier found shelter in a pleasant bay and was reflecting on the Festival of St. Lawrence celebrated on that date. The saint, born circa 215 in either Spain or Italy, died in 258 – martyred by fire. Cartier gave the river this saint's name.

Bridging The
Northumberland

"Ice boats were small, constructed as light as possible, consistent with strength and have runners on each side so they can be dragged over the snow and ice when necessary. Straps are attached to the sides and the boatmen and others have the other end fastened round their bodies either to assist in hauling or to enable them to get on the ice again should their feet drop through. Passengers have to pay $2.00 for the privilege of going with the crew and still have to assist in getting the boat along, but by paying a double fare they can stay on board during the whole crossing. When there is a strip of water everyone gets in the boat and it is rowed, and when they come to a field of ice it is hauled up and dragged along. "Lolly" – that is, a considerable body of snow in the water not frozen, or fine ground up ice – is what is by far the most dreaded, as in it neither can the boat be rowed nor can men walk."

– Past and Present of Prince Edward Island

Getting people, mail and goods across Northumberland Strait has been a challenge for Prince Edward Islanders since the first settlement. The Canadian government's guarantee of continuous and efficient year-round transportation service to the mainland was one of the reasons Prince Edward Island agreed to join Confederation in 1873. That service has taken many forms, from iceboats in the 1800s to the ferry service that operated year round until Confederation Bridge opened with much fanfare and hoopla In 1997.

Those who advocated the bridge over the existing ferry service used continuity and efficiency as two of their strongest arguments, promising that traffic would always be able to move on the bridge. It was a powerful argument.

The first time my husband and I got stuck on a ferry, it sailed up and down the strait for hours, waiting for the ice to shift enough

54

to get into the dock. True, it made us late, but someone had a guitar, others had decks of cards. Magazines and newspapers traded hands. People talked. We were warm, and the canteen always had food and coffee. As it got dark, parents went down to their cars for blankets and pillows, and little ones were put to bed on the couches or floors. There was a shared sense of adventure, reinforced by the sound of ice breaking beneath the hull and the sight of spotlights skimming the ice and water ahead to assist the crew to pick the best path through the ice fields.

There were also promises the bridge would save commuters money. It's less costly for a car with four adults to cross, but it's more expensive for one person.

Charlottetown was named by surveyor Samuel Holland as Charlotte Town, for Charlotte Sophia, the consort of King George III of England.

The bridge has had some growing pains:

- Truckers have experienced more delays than with the ferry due to high winds. Because there are as yet no facilities (washrooms, food and a warm place to wait), they are a tad upset! At the time of writing, a wind expert was being brought in, and catering trucks were being hired to provide coffee on the New Brunswick side.

- Folks do miss the ferries. They can get their fix during the summer by riding the Wood Islands service to Nova Scotia.

- There is no denying that 600 jobs on the ferries have been replaced by 14 on the bridge.

- The powers that be are worried that Islanders will start bringing huge quantities of canned beer to the island – where cans are a no-no. The PEI Liquor Control Commission has even placed ads in the newspapers warning Islanders that they are breaking the law if they bring more than 24 bottles (or cans) of beer, one quart of spirits or two litres of wine across the bridge. At least they haven't set up customs offices and begun car searches – yet.

- Tolls on the bridge increased before it had even been open a year. A sign of things to come?

The good news is:

- Cars don't have the same delays as trucks, so one can almost always drive on or off the island with no delays.
- Charlottetown to Moncton, a three-hour trip minimum and more often a five-hour journey by ferry, can easily be done via the bridge in one and a half hours – about 12 minutes to cross the bridge.

What are the "ingredients" for a bridge?
3 million tonnes of aggregates
340,000 cubic metres of concrete
543,000 tonnes of reinforcing steel
13,500 tonnes of post-tension cable
8,000 tonnes of miscellaneous metal fabrication
139,000 tonnes of asphalt paving

 Lake Utopia, near St. Andrews, New Brunswick, is the home of a legendary sea monster.

Before the Northumberland was spanned, another Maritime link held pride of place as an engineering marvel. Reversing tides jammed the Strait of Canso, dividing Cape Breton Island from mainland Nova Scotia, with drift ice well into late spring. This caused not only delays and traffic congestion but also great danger to steam-powered ferries which towed train barges. The building of the Causeway created an ice-free harbour on the Atlantic side with a permanent rail link, a 308-foot (94 metre) swing bridge, and a canal to enable ships to shorten their route to the St. Lawrence Seaway.

The harbour is one of the largest, deepest and safest ports on the continent. Bridging the Strait was no simple task. The 4500-foot (1371 metre) span of water, 217 feet (66 metres) deep, required more than 10 million tonnes of rock blasted from nearby Porcupine Mountain to complete the project.

On the August night when the Causeway was completed, an elderly lady who led her family in prayer added an oft-quoted gem: "And Thank God for having at last made Canada a part of Cape Breton."

ODD FACTS

At Magnetic Hill, just outside Moncton, cars appear to coast uphill thanks to an optical illusion provided by nature itself. It costs two bucks for staff to tell drivers to stop at the bottom of the steep hill, put the car in neutral and steer as it seems to climb back up the hill all on its own.

St. Andrews seems to have a tale around every corner, many of them based on characters who lived and worked in the town. One was Charles Briscoe, a dour individual who, in the 1820s, was reputed to be a member of the British royalty. Briscoe lived in a "salt-box," a New England-style home built in 1785 and still in use today. Apparently, he lived rather well, better than even his lucrative salary as harbourmaster would allow. He was, it is said, heard to mutter about the poor treatment he was getting and "if people only knew," implying that he was a man of importance. Papers found after his death showed that he was indeed the son of George III but was apparently given an income to keep quiet about his birth. Briscoe is buried near the old courthouse in St. Andrews.

About the same time, in 1822, a hot-tempered Scot by the name of Captain Christopher Scott lost his temper. The effects of his deed are still felt today. The good captain, you see, was a staunch Presbyterian. At a banquet, he was taunted about the fact that the "poor" Presbyterians couldn't afford to build a church. Pounding the table with his fists, Scott vowed to erect a fine church – the best in town. And he did. The Greenock church, named for Scott's home-town in Scotland, bears the image of a green oak tree, the symbol of Greenock, on the bell tower. The building was constructed with almost no nails or metal. Even the pulpit, of bird's-eye maple and mahogany, has no nails. It's a copy of the one in Greenock. Although future parishioners must have been glad of Scott's temper, it seems that he repented a little. He sent a large bronze remembrance plaque from Scotland showing the dove of peace bearing an olive branch in its beak – perhaps an apology to the people of St. Andrews for his bad temper.

More than 150,000 Irish immigrants arrived in Saint John between 1815 and 1850, many of them staying in the city, which may have reminded them of home. Or perhaps – after the tribulations of the voyage and the terrible conditions in the quarantine station of Partridge Island – they just couldn't face more travelling. Whatever the reason, the proportion of residents of Irish extraction in Saint John today exceeds that of any other large city in Canada.

Today's Maritimers come from all around the world. For instance, there's a sizable community of Lebanese extraction. But wherever they are from originally, without exception, they all now call the Maritimes "home."

CHAPTER 3

HOW WE WORK

"Nova Scotia is an
excellent poor man's
country, because
almost any man, in
any walk of industry,
by perseverance and
economy, can secure
the comforts of life."

– Joseph Howe,
July 31, 1834

Work. Hard, sometimes back-breaking work made the Maritimes, and Maritimers, what they are today. Now, you don't need to get out the violins, just appreciate that from the early days, when settlers waded ashore from sailing ships, hauling all their worldly goods, to the present-day Maritimers have been known as hard workers. Shoulder to the task, strong loyalties, pulling together to get a job done and looking after their own – those are the traits that a Maritimer make.

It began with hacking clearings, building cabins, pulling stumps and picking stones to clear fields. Once homes were established, these industrious folks turned their hands to earning livings and building communities. Churches, centres of not only religion but also much of the social life, and schools were built. Men settled into their chosen professions, often related to fishing, farming, mining, or lumbering. Women's work was centred on the home.

The unsung heroines of Canadian development were the women, the family caregivers. It was no easy task to do by hand things that we can't comprehend today. One of my earliest childhood memories is of my grandfather twisting the head off a chicken and bringing it to my grandmother to clean – still kicking. When my husband had to "do in" a randy rooster it was no quick flick of the wrist, he got a highpower rifle and they stalked each other around the barn for the good part of an hour before he shot it – through the comb. It flew to a neighbours, never to return! Good thing 'cause there was no way this chick was having any part of pluckin', cleanin' or anything else gross with any chicken.

Women's work was essential to family survival, yet it often went unrecognized. Our society would never have formed as it has without the contributions and unheralded accomplishments of the lady of the house. Maintaining a home in early Canada was a daunting task requiring the obvious and the not-so-obvious.

The obvious part was the labour of bringing children into the world: caring for them, nourishing and teaching them. Then there was the job of keeping house: cleaning, cooking, laundry, making clothing and linen, gardening and preserving food for the coming winter. The tradition of women doing a bit of selling or bartering became firmly established. Eggs, bread and preserves were sold, and sewing and other services brought "pin money" and a small measure of independence.

The not so obvious part was recognized by the rulers in Europe. They understood that women were vital in establishing a permanent white population and in bringing proper social and religious values to the New World. Mothers demanded that society provide for their children relative safety, good morals and education. They were responsible for much of the community work, contributing hours to all manner of projects for the good of all.

Sweden is Nova Scotia's largest investor.

Most pioneer women were married and worked in the home. The few single women either depended on family or worked as servants. As the years went by, a few occupations became acceptable for women: dressmaking and domestic service came first, and teaching eventually became a vocation suitable for young women. Wages were low, but the status of female teacher was higher than that of other occupations. Nursing, like teaching, developed into a women's profession at a time when social needs coincided with individual women's search for a "respectable" career. Women had an important role in family businesses, and they often had a role in the community as healers, relying on herbs and common sense, but their standing in the medical community was at the bottom of the hierarchy. As medicine itself began to progress, men essentially became diagnosticians, whereas women did the grunt work.

One of the earliest English-Canadian hospitals, located in Halifax in the 18th century, was operated by an inspector and surgeon general who was paid a guinea a day. The matron of the hospital, Sarah Dunlop, carried a huge load. She would change bandages, clean wounds, administer medicines, apply poultices, arrange food for patients and keep the building maintained and clean. She received no salary.

EARLY TRADERS

Much as we "European descendants" might like to take credit, Maritime commerce did not begin when our ancestors arrived. Native peoples who lived along the rivers and seacoasts used their big canoes to trade, raid and probably visit the neighbours for a gossip, travelling as far as New England and Newfoundland. Glad it was them heading out on that open water, and not me – the sea-sick queen! Records show that sometime in the 1500s the trade of weapons was taking place – sort of a long-lasting "guy thing." Food, shelter and clothing came from the land and sea around them. The things they made – the experts call this their "material culture" – show an ingenious use of natural materials from plants, animals and minerals. Of course, once trading started it continued, and you can bet the gals were right in there!

Traditionally, Micmac wove baskets from reeds, roots and shoots of alder and other shrubs. From 1800 to World War II families with an entrepreneurial bent earned a living by making and selling baskets. Ash and maple were favoured by skilled craftspeople, whose magic fingers wove an amazing variety of useful and decorative baskets and novelties to sell.

Basket making is an art form that has been reestablished, and many fine baskets are again being sold in places such as Prince Edward Island's Lennox Island.

Beginning about 1650, women made birch boxes decorated with porcupine quills to sell to Europeans. Beautiful panels for local furniture makers, boxes, mats and baskets were decorated with quills coloured using plant dyes and later synthetic dyes, which produced brighter colours.

Europeans were quick to recognize Micmac skill, particularly with birchbark, a wonderful material that can be peeled from trees in large sheets that are tough, waterproof and insect repellent. When warmed and dampened, it is easily cut, folded and sewn into bowls, moose calls and wigwams; the Micmac even boiled water in birch-bark containers. Most importantly, it was used to make canoes.

INVENTIONS & OTHER GREAT THINGS

Making significant contributions to the world has become somewhat of a tradition among skilled Maritimers.

When Nova Scotia let Dr. Abraham Gesner go from his job as provincial geologist in 1842, the province did the world a favour. Trained in medicine, with a love for geology, he set up Canada's first museum and extended the geological survey of New Brunswick. He also invented. In 1846 Gesner demonstrated a substance that he called "kerosene" (a name coined from the Greek words for wax and oil) in Charlottetown. The distillation process was patented in 1854. Although it tended to be a bit smelly, the first "coal oil" burned a much brighter and cleaner flame than whale or seal oil or tallow candles. Gesner was sometimes called the father of night life! A forerunner of today's petrochemical industry, good old Gesner still had his problems. Although he invented the oil before a Scottish chemist did, he lost the race to the patent office and had to pay royalties for the right to use his own process. Just goes to show that government cutbacks are not new and that benefits can sometimes be measured in strange and wonderful ways.

Newfoundlander Frederic Newton Gisborne laid the first submarine telegraph cable off North America between Cape Tormentine, New Brunswick, and Carleton Head, Prince Edward Island, in 1852. Using an insulated wire that was impervious to saltwater corrosion, he began experiments that led to the establishment of telegraphic communications between Europe and North America.

The story of early radio in Canada would make a great miniseries. Radio pioneer Guglielmo Marconi received the first transatlantic wireless message on a hilltop in St. John's, Newfoundland, from Cornwall, England, on December 12, 1901. Now Newfoundlanders, it seems, saw Marconi as a threat to their cable companies as stock began to plummet. Instead of drawing Marconi into their fold, they claimed exclusive rights to telegraph communications from "the Rock" and gave Marconi the old heave-ho. The government of Canada was delighted and offered Marconi $80,000 to set up his operations in Glace Bay, Cape Breton. He built a wireless station that connected Canada and England. It all led to Canada's first electronics company, the Marconi Wireless Telegraph Company of Canada. Established under a federal charter, it began what became an excellent tradition of government support for quality Canadian radio. Marconi shared the Nobel Prize for physics in 1909.

In 1910 MacKay Motorcar Manufacturer in Amherst, Nova Scotia, was a North American leader.

John Fraser of Pictou, Nova Scotia, was the first person in North America to use a diving suit and helmet in the first commercial underwater salvage operation. In 1842 Fraser brought the technology home from the coast of Germany, where he had been doing some undersea salvage work for Lloyd's. He and diving partner Alexander Munro salvaged 35 cannon from the HMS *Mallabar* off Cape Bear, Prince Edward Island. Seems there wasn't enough money in the diving business, because the partners did no further known underwater salvage. Or maybe the cumbersome gear (120 pounds (54.5 kg) of lead in the suit) turned them off. Their deepest dive was reportedly 36 feet (about 10 metres) in Pictou Harbour.

A Yarmouth sea captain came up with the notion of the screw propeller in 1833. Powered by a hand crank, his small boat amazed local citizens when it moved without oar, paddle or sail. His invention, combined with advances in steam power, allowed ships to dispense with cumbersome paddle wheels.

The first and only all-steel sailing schooner built in Canada, the *James William*, was built in New Glasgow in 1908 by James Carmichael, the brother-in-law of Captain George Rogers MacKenzie, a renowned Bluenose shipbuilder and skipper.

Some of the greatest inventions are things that ordinary individuals rarely hear about, let alone understand or appreciate. Take the variable-pitch propeller, invented by Wallace Rupert Turnbull, of Saint John, New Brunswick. Without it the air transportation industry could not have gotten off the ground. Called "one of the most important developments in the whole history of aviation," it allowed a pilot to alter the length and slant of propeller blades while in motion, thereby increasing efficiency. Before 1920 aircraft could not carry heavy payloads that required extra fuel. Propellers of the time were well suited for takeoff, but they could not be adjusted once the plane was in flight. Turnbull's invention allowed aircraft companies to earn money for the first time and thus to survive without direct government subsidies. New aircraft could be developed, and an air transportation industry formed.

A beautiful car with gull-like wings put New Brunswick on the automotive map, if only briefly. Now extinct, if that is the right word, Bricklins were built in Saint John, but only 1,880 cars were produced before the company failed. Named for their designer and promoter, and sponsored by the late Richard Hatfield, then premier of the province, Bricklins found their way all over the world, a toy for moneyed admirers of the sleek auto. But there were problems, especially with the doors (the wings), which on occasion would not open. The moneyed did not appreciate having to climb out of the small windows. On other days, the doors would not close – equally embarrassing. These days about the only place you'll see a Bricklin is in a museum.

SETTING THE WORLD TICKING HIS WAY

Sir Sandford Fleming of Halifax, Canada's foremost railway surveyor and construction engineer, became the chief surveyor and later the chief engineer of the first railway between Halifax, St. John and Quebec City in the 1860s. He went on to be a valuable contributor to the Canadian Pacific Railway and to the laying of a telecommunications cable from Canada to Australia in 1902. But it was his penchant for keeping things on time that put his name in history books.

When working on the railway, Fleming was appalled by the confusion in early railway timetables, caused by clocks in the stations across Upper and Lower Canada being set a little ahead or behind those in towns a few miles west or east. He wrote a pamphlet in which he outlined a plan to carve the world into 24 time zones; by his scheme, all who lived in one of these sections would set their clocks to the same standard time and change their watches only every few hundred miles. Plain citizens and knowing scientists derided Fleming, just as they laughed at Alexander Graham Bell, but eight years later, after presenting his system of standard, or mean, time to the International Prime Meridian Conference in Washington in 1884, his system of International Standard Time – still in use today – was adopted.

Fleming also designed the first Canadian postage stamp, the three-penny beaver, issued in 1851.

Best known as the inventor of the telephone, Alexander Graham Bell contributed so much more it simply boggles the mind. As a teacher, inventor, innovator, inspirer of others and most of all humanitarian, Bell bridged the world between sound and silence, teaching deaf people to speak and pursuing ideas from transmitting sound on light waves to developing treadle-powered graphophones. He grew up with a father whose goal was to create visible speech so that peoples of all languages, including sign language, could communicate. His mother and his wife were deaf. Bell wanted to help people speak and became one of the outstanding figures of his generation in the education of the deaf.

 It is believed that the first dial telephones in Canada came into use in Sydney Mines, Nova Scotia, in 1907.

In 1885 Bell and his wife, Mabel, visited Baddeck on Cape Breton. It was love at first sight. They established a home and a 600-

acre estate, regularly spending a substantial part of the year at Beinn Bhreagh. By the time the Bells arrived in Baddeck, the success of the telephone had freed him from the need to earn a living. He continued his busy routine of experimentation and analysis, his imagination and wide-ranging curiosity leading him into areas such as sound transmission, medicine, aeronautics, marine engineering and space-frame construction.

Aeronautical work was a large part of his life on Cape Breton, from early kite-flying experiments to the success of the Silver Dart in 1909. This achievement was the result of Bell's association with four young men (Casey Baldwin, J. A. Douglas McCurdy, Lieutenant Thomas Selfridge and Glenn Curtiss) in the Aerial Experimental Association (AEA), formed in 1907. The first recorded flight in the British Empire of a heavier-than-air machine took place at Baddeck when Thomas Selfridge was lifted into the air on December 6, 1907, in a tetrahedral kite, the *Cygnet,* designed by Bell. McCurdy flew Bell's aircraft, the *Silver Dart,* at Baddeck in 1909. It was the first powered flight in the British Empire.

In 1874 John Hamilton, a black Fredericton railway worker, invented the first known snowplow for trains.

In later years, Bell and Baldwin turned to experiments with hydrofoil craft that culminated in the HD-4, which set a world speed record in 1919 – an unprecedented 70.86 miles per hour – and paved the way for hydrofoil development.

These activities had a significant impact on the economic and social life of Baddeck. The estate provided work for men and women both in traditional occupations and in jobs connected with Bell's experiments, such as the production of thousands of tetrahedral cells for his massive kites.

Mabel Bell played a vital role in her husband's career, providing him with both financial and moral support to pursue his diverse interests. It was Mabel who inspired, founded and funded the AEA, which achieved heavier-than-air flight. She managed the estate and was deeply involved in village life, helping to establish the local public library and Home and School Association as well as a reading club for young women.

STEEL TOWN

Although Sydney is commonly called "steel town," Pictou County in Nova Scotia was actually the birthplace of steel in Canada and one of Canada's earliest heavy-industry centres during the late 1800s. Two New Glasgow blacksmiths, Graham Fraser and Forrest MacKay, made steel at the Nova Scotia Steel Company in 1883. Other attempts at steel making had been unsuccessful. The pig iron needed to make steel was imported from Scotland until Fraser founded the New Glasgow Iron, Coal and Railway Company and produced it from local coal, iron ore and limestone. Fraser also built North America's first coal-washing plant to reduce sulphur content.

The first iron rail lines manufactured in North America came out of Albion Steel in Pictou County. They were used in tramways prior to 1839, allowing coal to be hauled by horse-drawn rail cars. Albion went on to produce three steam locomotives. One, the Sampson, is on display in New Glasgow. It is North America's oldest surviving steam locomotive, so famous it visited the 1893 World's Fair in Chicago.

The first all-steel bridge in Canada was built across the reversing falls at St. John in 1884.

RETAIL WIZARDS & GIANTS OF COMMERCE

Little did folks suspect that a wee lad born to humble beginnings in Bouctouche, New Brunswick, would grow up to build a business empire that made him one of the wealthiest people in the world when he died in 1993. K. C. Irving made most of his money in oil, gas and timber. He began his career in his hometown with a small gas station. He even slept at the station so that he could leap out of bed at any hour to pump gas. Soon he moved on to Saint John, where oil refineries and the Irving headquarters are located today. The familiar red-and-blue logo of Irving service stations now pops up every few miles in New England and in Quebec and Ontario, and Irving's descendants have taken the empire into other areas of production, including Cavendish Farm frozen french fries.

The father of door-to-door sales, Alfred C. Fuller, was born in Welsford, Nova Scotia, in 1885. Hard times drove young Alfred to stay with his sister in Connecticut, and in 1906 he began making brushes at night and selling them door to door during the day. Those brushes, made in his sister's cellar, were the foundation of a company so widespread that the Fuller Brush sales rep was known across North America. Movies, *The Fuller Brush Man,* with Red Skelton, and *The Fuller Brush Woman,* with Lucille Ball, kept the legend alive. A good product and an image that is still envied by retailers kept Fuller Brush at the top of the heap for years. Headquarters are in Canada, and the brushes are now sold more by women than by men.

An out-of-work carpenter, John William Sobey, began operating a horse-driven meat cart in 1907, creating a business that would grow to a mighty enterprise of 120 stores in six provinces, grossing over $3 billion a year. Sobey was 38. Just two years earlier, he, his wife and their young son, Frank, had moved to Stellarton to work build-ing shafts with the Acadia Coal Company.

John's business slowly grew, but it was young Frank who would oversee most of the growth and success. He had a knack for business, finding it exciting and rewarding at an age when schoolmates were still playing cowboys and ball. Frank made a $100 profit in Grade 8 by buying shares of Canada Cement. It was probably not coinciden-tal that his public school education immediately ceased, and at age 16 he enrolled in a business college. There he acquired the practical skills that would serve him so well in life: typing, accounting and especially calculating percentages, because "It's the percentage of the selling price you worked on, not the cost."

Soon Frank put his own mark on the family business. He persuaded his father to expand from selling meat and a few locally grown vegetables into a full line of groceries in 1924. In 1925, visiting Boston with his wife, Irene, he encountered the cash register, a revolutionary idea in retailing. Unlike his father's store, which offered charge accounts, the American food chains accepted cash only. The first self-serve, all-cash Sobeys supermarket opened its automatic doors in August 1947 – it was an immediate success. Cecil McLean, the supermarket's first meat manager, recalled: "There must have been a hundred people just standing around watching them doors."

Rapid expansion in the Maritimes took place over the next three decades, and Frank's three sons joined the management team. Sobeys grocery stores were opened in Newfoundland, Quebec and Ontario. By 1971 Frank's sons had taken the helm: Bill as president, David as executive vice-president and Donald as head of the growing investment company Empire Inc. Frank still oversaw activities as chairman of the board. Now in its 90th year of service, Sobeys remains proudly Atlantic Canadian.

Back in 1898, a Nova Scotian company became a byword among the hardy sourdoughs of the Yukon Klondike trail. Stanfield's "Unshrinkable" Underwear was a must for miners, who could find no substitute for the warm, heavy, woolly underwear made in Truro. "Unshrinkables" were just one of the achievements of one of the oldest manufacturers of quality underwear in Canada. It all began in 1855. After immigrating to Canada, Charles E. Stanfield, along with his brother-in-law, established several knitting mills. In 1906 their Truro Knitting Mills got a new name and incorporated as Stanfield's Limited, continuing to operate on the same site. And there they remain, with a factory outlet. The company does more than any other in the region to keep people cozy and comfy.

During World War I, the mill manufactured wool blankets, knitting yarns and cloth, and it perfected the wool used for underwear. Cotton combinations were introduced in the early 1920s, and the first synthetic fibre was put into women's undergarments in 1926. This rayon cloth was referred to as nova silk by the firm. Knit briefs began to replace woven underwear. In the late 1930s, Stanfield's entered the athletic shirt and short market and was the first to package these items in cellophane bags. Winter shirts and long underwear were introduced in the early 1940s, and T-shirts, along with thermal underwear, appeared in the 1950s.

Stanfield's now employs over 650 people – a far cry from the 17 employees in 1896.

DISTAFF ENTREPRENEUR

Although only a small portion of the early European population of the Maritimes was engaged in trade (most were farming, fishing or soldiering), they had a strong influence on the development of the nation. Among those first entrepreneurs were many married women who acted as partners, often running businesses at home while husbands were away on business trips. So common was this practice that women in business were an accepted part of the culture. Family businesses are still a strong part of Maritime life. So too are both small and large operations owned by women.

Among the first businesswomen to gain recognition in Canada was Françoise-Marie Jacquelin, Madame de la Tour. In the 1600s, Charles de la Tour and his rival Charles D'Aulnay were involved in a struggle over a large chunk of what is now New Brunswick. The land had been granted to de la Tour by the king of France, who apparently forgot what he had done and gave the same real estate to D'Aulnay. De la Tour established trade with New England and found coal in 1643, which he sold in Boston. While monsieur was away on business, madame ran things at home.

So bitter was the dispute that, when it came time to sell their year's furs, Charles stayed in Canada to defend his claim while Jacquelin took furs to France to sell. Task accomplished, she loaded the ship with provisions and sent it home while she went to Paris to defend their land rights. She was unsuccessful in the French court. No one knows just what happened there – D'Aulnay had gotten there before her – but speculation is that prejudice weighed heavily against the former actress, who had dared to go to Acadia to marry a man she had never seen, having been chosen by his agent for her "good physique." Or perhaps the all-male court was not at ease with a successful woman.

Jacquelin hastily returned to Canada, where she found her family, workers and soldiers under siege in their fort. Stealing into the stronghold, she sent Charles to Boston to seek help. She defended the fort against D'Aulnay's attack and could have held out until help arrived if not betrayed by one of the hired men.

D'Aulnay captured the fort, and despite Jacquelin's pleading he hanged all the men and boys while she looked on, a noose around her own neck. She was not hanged that day but was imprisoned and found dead a few days later, undoubtedly executed by some method more "genteel" than public hanging.

THE COOPERATIVE WAY

"It is the Hungry Thirties in Nova Scotia – where the Twenties were nothing to shout about. Fishing smacks lie rotting on the beaches because the world has no money to buy fish; miners on relief hunch dispiritedly on the doorsteps of weather-beaten shacks, staring blankly at the thin-ribbed youngsters who play in the dusty roads. The working men without work are almost without hope.

A black-garbed priest goes among them and he murmurs no platitudes. He does offer them a new slogan: 'You can beat your poverty through education if you learn how to co-operate."

– Gerald Anglin
Canada Unlimited, 1948

A potent force in the development of cooperatives in Canada, Moses Coady, born in Margaree, Nova Scotia, in 1882, was an integral part of the Antigonish movement that developed in the late 1920s as an attempt to move the region toward self-sufficiency. Through educational and self-help campaigns, the movement pushed forward the ideas of cooperatives and credit unions as means for people to take control of the local economy and become, as Coady's popular book was entitled, *Masters of Their Own Destiny.* The book, published in 1939, has been translated into seven languages and is still in print.

Coady's ultimate dream was to establish an international institute for the development of cooperatives. He died in 1959, his dream unrealized, but a few months later the Coady Institute was established at St. Francis Xavier University in Antigonish. The institute was a pioneer in the development of cooperatives, and in the 1960s it educated many of the "fathers and mothers" of co-op movements in other countries. Its primary focus is to strengthen existing organizations in the developing world, and its work has expanded beyond promoting cooperatives and credit unions to exploring other means of organizing people to take control of the local economy.

Down Underground

"The most important thing to come out of a mine is a miner."
— *from the Westray Inquiry*

Since 1670, when a certain "Captain Poulet" first found coal, Cape Breton miners have been identified with the coal and steel industries of the Royal Island. In 1672 a book by Nicholas Denys, published in France, mentioned these coal discoveries. It took 25 years before the French found surface coal at Louisbourg, and not until 1720 was a shaft sunk at Morien.

In March 1925, Cape Breton coal miners received $3.65 in daily wages and had been working part time for more than three years. They burned company coal to heat company houses illuminated by company electricity. Their families drank company water, were indebted to the company "Pluck Me" store and were financially destitute, as evidenced by the company "bob-tailed sheet." Local clergy spoke of children clothed in flour sacks and dying of starvation from the infamous "four-cent meal." The miners had fought continuously for an eight-hour day and a living wage. Although workers' conditions were deplorable, the company demanded that the miners take even more cuts. The United Mine Workers of America attempted to negotiate improvements for mine workers. The company fought back with further cuts, going so far as to cut power and water to the town, including the hospital, full of sick children. Drunken company police rode down children in the schoolyard.

Cape Breton coal mine tunnels extend far out under the sea.

The battle lines were drawn. An army of angry miners, determined to restore electricity, marched on the plant. When the air cleared, it was discovered that William Davis, a 37-year-old UMWA bother, had been fatally shot. His funeral drew more than 5,000 people who came to pay tribute to a working man. From that day forward, it was said, no miner would work the black seam on Davis Day.

> "There is no finer person on this planet than the working man who carries his lunch can deep into the bowels of the earth. Far beneath the ocean he works the black seam; an endless ribbon of steel his only link to fresh air and blue skies. The steel rails symbolize a miner's life, half buried underground, half reaching toward his final reward."
>
> – *Stephen J. Drake,*
> *President of UMWA District 26*

A coal mine explosion at Springhill, Nova Scotia, trapped 174 miners on October 23, 1958. Rescue workers brought 81 men out on the first day, 12 on October 30 and seven more on November 1. Seventy-four miners died underground. The extent of the tragedy began to sink in after the rescue of the last seven men.

The name of a black miner became synonymous with courage and strength of will. Maurice Ruddick was one of the few black men who worked in the Springhill collieries. The 46-year-old father of 12 was a well-liked member of the crew who loved to sing as he worked, and he became known as the "Singing Miner." When the most severe "bump" in North American mining swept through No. 2, causing a massive cave-in that instantly crushed 73 men to death, Ruddick felt his way over rubble and bodies until he came upon a huddle of survivors. A group of seven formed as more men, limping, crawling and stunned by toxic gasses, joined one another in a small clearing. In the dark, hungry and dehydrated, the entombed men waited anxiously, wondering whether they would ever be found. As they waited, Ruddick sang hymns. His singing kept their hopes alive.

When rescuers found them, Ruddick was singing at the top of his lungs. He was credited with keeping the others alive, making headlines around the world. The governor of Georgia invited the survivors to recuperate in the sunny South. All was fine until he learned that Ruddick was black – and Ruddick learned that Georgia was segregated!

Ruddick was named Citizen of the Year and received many honours. He once told legislators that being introduced to Parliament was the second greatest thing that had ever happened to him. "Getting rescued was the first."

J. Frank Willis gave the first on-the-spot news coverage of rescue operations after the Moose River Mine disaster in Nova Scotia. The explosion on April 12, 1936, trapped three men in the mine, and a Canadian Radio-Broadcasting Corporation team headed by Willis gave non-stop reports on the incident for 69 hours until two survivors were brought to the surface. The broadcasts were picked up by 650 stations in the United States and 58 in Canada and began an era of live, sensationalist journalism.

The unique Miners Museum, a centennial project, is above an old coal mine, the Ocean Deeps Colliery. Guided by retired miners, visitors descend into the bona fide mine, protected by traditional gear, including a miner's hat and lamp. The day I visited the mine, the vocal group "Men of the Deep" were crooning a tune for a television special – what a bonus!

THAR'S GOLD
IN THEM THAR HILLS

Although the Maritimes big Goldrush occurred in 1861 when the cry of "Gold!" rang out in the town of Sherbrooke it was actually sighted as early as 1578 when the explorer Sir Humphry Gilbert was given a patent to search for gold and silver in the New World. The names of villages Brad d'Or, Cape d'Or or Jeddore (Jet d'Or) indicated French settlers may well have found their own version of treasure.

In the 1830s labourers building roads in Nova Scotia found gold, but did not realize what it was. They actually whittled the gold with their knives during mealtimes. A captain the Royal Welsh Fusiliers panned gold at Gold River in 1840, and W. Brooks, a farmer from Lawrencetown, claimed to have found gold when repairing a dam on his land. His father told him to "drop his nonsense, go on with his work and pitch the rubbish away." Eleven years later, Brooks again discovered gold and the area was declared the Lawrencetown Gold District. Gold was found in Tangiers, Musquodoboit, Fort Clarence in Halifax Harbour (where the oil refinery lies today), The Ovens, Wine Harbour, Waverley, Country Harbour, Isaacs Harbour and at Mooseland.

Now Mooseland may seem an unlikely spot for a gold rush, but the region's first of four "rushes" took place here when, in late May 1860, John Gerrish Pulsiver found gold in a quartz bolder.

You can get a feel for the "golden age" of the 1800s by visiting the Sherbrooke Village Restoration Area. The farming/fishing village became an energetic mining camp and, by 1869, 19 mining companies had joined that rush. They would prosper for the next 20 years.

Gold was big news in those days. The Klondike gold rush lured tens of thousands of drifters and dreamers to the Yukon, whipped into gold fever frenzy by sensationalist journalism in the newspapers. Among the stampeders were a few Maritimers who made a place for themselves in the history books. Robert Douglas Henderson of Halifax is often called the true discoverer of Klondike gold. He urged George Carmack to prospect the tributaries of Indian River, a tip that led to the discovery of gold in Bonanza Creek. The rotten lot didn't even share news of the strike with Henderson! New Brunswick's "Big Alex" McDonald introduced the "lay" system, hiring others to mine his property for a percentage. He reinvested in more and more land, becoming very rich, famous on three continents and even met with the pope.

Gold mining has almost come to a standstill in Nova Scotia due to sagging gold prices and the cost of production. However, Fredericton-based EMR Microwave Technology now claims it has a new way to extract precious metal from hard rock. Yup, they "nuke" it! Microwaved gold – *hmmmm!* Having once disintegrated a sausage and blown up the plate, I'm a little leery about gold in the "mic." But, the way the price of gold keeps going up it might just be the catalyst that is needed to kickstart our fifth Gold Rush.

Mining Firsts

Maritime miners were the first off the mark in many ways:
- The world's first mine flooded to produce thermal energy was at Springhill, Nova Scotia, where a depth of 3.2 kilometres produces 20° Celsius water.
- Glace Bay miners were the first to wear self-contained breathing apparatus in mine rescue work in 1906.
- The first pit-mouth coal power plant in North America opened at the Chignecto mine in 1907.
- Saint John, noted as having the largest oil refinery in Canada, was also the site of the construction of the first Canadian semisubmersible oil rig for offshore use, at Saint John Shipbuilding & Dry Dock Company. It's also the location of Canaport, the first deepwater port in Canada specifically designed for supertankers.
- Southwest of Sable Island, production of Canada's first offshore oil began at the Cohasset-Panuke oil fields in 1992. The crude was known as Scotian Light. Sounds like a beer. These days Sable Island is in the news as a future provider of natural gas.

Living Off The Land

Traditional farming has been and continues to be an important economic and social contributor to Maritime life. Always innovative, Maritimers make many and varied uses of the land base. For instance, it was a need for medicinal herbs that caused Louis Hébert to become the first Canadian farmer. Coming to Acadia in 1604, he helped sick settlers by using the same remedies he had used in France, where he had been a court apothecary as well as an attorney.

There are about 400 maple syrup producers in New Brunswick, with nearly 1.2 million taps producing 817,000 litres of syrup worth $6-7 million annually. Once the syrup is bottled and ready, seasonal pancake suppers are held wherever there are sugar bushes.

Nova Scotia is the world's largest exporter of lobsters, Christmas trees, gypsum and wild blueberries.

In the past 25 years, the number of cows in Prince Edward Island has decreased by 33 percent, but milk production has increased by 75 percent due to better farming practices. The province has gained an international reputation for its advanced dairy breeding, resulting in exports as far away as Mexico, Korea and Morocco. The University of Prince Edward Island has launched space age dairy research; for instance, a 1997 experiment on Mir Space Station created artificial proteins that increase milk production.

The Lings were the first Chinese farmers in Nova Scotia. How Ling came to Halifax from New Glasgow via Winnipeg in 1918, at the end of World War I. Kidnaped from China at the age of nine, Toy Sing was brought to Canada, where she adopted the name Chong. She worked in British Columbia as a domestic servant until, at age 16, she married How Ling in an arranged marriage. The Lings ran a cattle, oat and wheat farm and a laundry in New Glasgow. In 1925 they moved to Brookside to farm, then to Gottingen Street in

Halifax, where they ran a Chinese chicken and vegetable farm. In 1942 they moved again, this time to Upper Water Street to open the Imperial Café near the present-day ferry terminal. Mary Ling was born in 1933 on the family farm. She recalls the RCMP raiding the house looking for opium. Suspicions may have been raised because Mary's father smoked his tobacco in a water pipe. Mary went on to operate Mary's Bread Basket in Halifax.

"Up west" in Prince Edward Island, visitors are impressed by fine Victorian homes. Ask about their origin and you are likely to be told, "Oh, that's a fox house." It all began in 1896 when Charles Dalton and Robert Oulton found some silver fox pups – a rare find indeed. Red foxes were common; silver foxes were a treasure. Realizing the value of the find, they quietly began a breeding program. The two were ideal partners: Oulton was skilled with the foxes, Dalton with the business. It was a match that led to the establishment of the Canadian fox fur industry. Silver fox fur found ready buyers willing to pay high prices for the luxurious pelts.

A small group of island entrepreneurs, led by Dalton, kept tight control of the industry, never selling breeding stock off the island. The industry was worth $20 million a year to Prince Edward Island. Eventually, in 1910, someone broke ranks and sold a breeding pair "away," thus opening up the industry. Prosperity continued for three more decades. Dalton was just one who made a fortune. In the 1920s, the industry represented 17 percent of the economy. It is said that one breeding pair sold for $35,000. The Canadian National Silver Fox Breeders Association located its headquarters in Summerside. Today the International Fox Museum and Hall of Fame keeps the memory of the glory days alive.

The industry collapsed in the 1940s. The market was flooded with fox pelts. A few individuals still keep silver foxes as a hobby, striving to keep the breed alive. And every so often a silver fox will be spotted in the wild, for many breeders simply opened cage doors and freed their stock when the industry collapsed.

Living From The Sea

The Maritimes are ideally situated for world trade. They also have a fishing industry right at their door. But there have been drastic changes in how we earn our living from the sea over the past 350 years.

Cod do not swim in the great numbers they once did – today a moratorium almost totally restricts landing what was the mainstay of the Atlantic fishing industry. And, in spite of strict regulations, many of the species are no longer abundant. In fact, the Atlantic Cod was placed on the endangered species list in 1998. Fishing is restricted to seasons and districts to ensure the future of wild stocks. Lobster, for example, can only be fished for in May and June in most of Prince Edward Island. Before May the ice is too thick to safely allow boats into the water. By July the lobster are starting to moult and cannot be fished because Canada has taken a policy that only hard-shelled lobster be sold to ensure both the future of the species and the quality of meat going to the marketplace. These seasons differ throughout the region, ensuring that lobster is harvested somewhere in Atlantic Canada year round.

If you see a fenced-in area on the Fundy shore of New Brunswick that looks like a crude fort, you have found a lobster pound, in which live lobsters are held in natural seawater until they can be taken to the marketplace. These enclosures can hold as much as 6 million pounds (2.7 million kg) of lobster a year, worth upward of $20 million.

In shallow bays, criss-crossed sticks in the water or people standing in boats manipulating long tongs, or oyster rakes, signify the harvesting of oysters. The most famous are the Malpeques from Prince Edward Island. Lines for collecting spat (baby oysters) are held by those sticks. The little fellows cling to the lines until moved to oyster beds at the bottom of the bay. Three or four years later, when the oyster is about four inches long and has a hard bumpy shell, it is ready to eat. The oysters are then taken to a processor where they are graded and packed for shipment around the world.

Clam shelling, or shucking, requires expertise. An experienced shucker can pry open the shell and cut out the meat at a rate of about 700 clams per hour. The meat is dropped into buckets and later fried, a delicacy for which the region is known. Several small clam operations can be found on the New Brunswick side of the Bay of Fundy.

So can Connors sardine factory, the largest sardine plant anywhere. Black's Harbour, where the main Connors plant is located, has been a real company town. Just about everything – including the local dragstrip, theatre and even the majority of the housing (rented at rates we all dream of) – has belonged to the company. Connors has been known to can 2 million cases, that would be over a billion sardines, in a year.

Another important fish-processing industry, near St. Andrews, New Brunswick, has the advantage of being closer to Peru, via the Panama Canal, than to Vancouver. Strange that Pacific tuna makes its way into cans in an Atlantic canning factory.

Going to the ice floes to watch the seals has become a growth tourism industry in Prince Edward Island. An early spring in 1998 caused an estimated herd of 500,000 seals to take to the ice between North Cape, Prince Edward Island, and New Brunswick. One of the tourists to take to the ice was a 102-year-old woman from Ontario.

FAMILY LIFE AT SEA

The sea is often assumed to be an all-male environment. However, in the late 1800s, women and children appeared in more visible numbers aboard Canadian sailing vessels – far more than on ships of other nations. Following a husband or father to sea transformed the ideal Victorian family. Heavy loads of laundry, often done by servants or other family members at home, became the task of the captain's wife. Deprived of playmates, children found friends in shipboard pets and sometimes helped the crew. Wives also witnessed up close the harsh reality of managing undercrewed ships and underpaid men. Several witnessed violent mutiny first-hand, and others were clearly frightened by the seamen working around them.

Other women, such as Emma Spicer, found themselves acting as supplemental crew when stewards left or when injuries called for their doctoring skills. The seagoing Spicer family was unique in that it produced four notable captains in a single generation. The parents, Jacob and Mary, were substantial landowners with Loyalist roots from Spencer's Island in the Bay of Fundy. Of their nine children who grew to adulthood, almost all chose the sea. Daughters Antoinette and Blanche married captains, with whom they travelled; both lost their husbands at sea. The Spicers' sons – George, Dewis, Johnson and Edmund, the "big four" – made distinguished international careers as masters of some of Nova Scotia's largest vessels. They held shares in each other's ships and took turns in command.

As shipping declined at the turn of the century, the Spicers invested in lumbering and farming. Dewis retired to the large family home. This home held the family's unique collection of seagoing possessions and documents from three generations before it was sold to collector Harold Lister to keep it intact. Today these artifacts can be seen at the Maritime Museum of the Atlantic in Halifax.

Women were not permitted to command vessels in the 19th century. It was not until 1938 that Molly Kool of the Bay of Fundy became one of the first female captains in the Western world.

Bessie Hall studied navigation and ship handling from her father, Captain Joseph Hall, of the barque Rothsay. Despite the prohibition against female command, she showed that she could not only navigate and command a ship but also do so under remarkable circumstances. In 1870 smallpox struck the already short-handed vessel, leaving Captain Hall and his officers helplessly sick. After meeting with the crew, Bessie took command and for six weeks navigated through gales and contrary winds to their destination at Liverpool, England. Although known among mariners, her accomplishments were not widely publicized at the time. After a final voyage in 1871, Bessie left the sea to marry and settled in Annapolis, Nova Scotia.

Women appeared in small but consistent numbers on Nova Scotian sailing ships as stewardesses and cook's helpers. Often wives or daughters of stewards or cooks, they were paid as crew. Unlike the members of a captain's family, they rarely left diaries or photos. Historians have traced their careers through crew lists and wage agreements. Not surprisingly, considering their outnumbered status, unglamorous work and low pay, they sometimes challenged refined Victorian notions of female behaviour with formidable profanity and an assertiveness that was not afraid to threaten an officer with a black eye.

OUR GUIDING LIGHTS

Mariners face many hazards as they navigate the coastline. In darkness and during raging storms, what sight could be more welcome than a beacon of light signalling land's edge.

Lighthouses are one member of a family of navigational aids that includes buoys, foghorns, markers, radar and satellite systems, all vital in ships past dangers. Lighthouses are entrenched in the culture and hearts of Maritimers.

Lighthouses have evolved from simple bonfires to electronic beacons. A few hundred years ago, fishers used lights along the shore to guide them home and to help them avoid dangerous waters. Bonfires evolved into flares that sat atop wooden towers, allowing sailors to navigate from farther out to sea. Then the ubiquitous Dr. Abraham Gesner demonstrated his kerosene lamps in Charlottetown homes in 1841. Kerosene became the main source of energy in lighthouses across Canada until petroleum and acetylene lamps became popular at the turn of the century. By the 1960s, electricity had replaced oil. The costly and complex lenses used with oil and kerosene are no longer needed. Electric lamps are cheaper both to buy and to maintain. Electric motors replaced hand-wound spring motors that rotated the lenses and covers to give the lights their sequence of flashes. Information on emergency fuel supply, beacon visibility and foghorn operation is now electronically relayed to the coast guard.

Lighthouses are still a popular part of our landscape, but as they become less important for navigation their use is changing. When no longer needed, they can be converted to hotels, museums or restaurants. Sadly, they are sometimes torn down or abandoned. Lighthouse societies, though, help to ensure that the future of Maritime lighthouses remains bright.

Sambro Light, off Nova Scotia, built in 1758, is North America's oldest standing lighthouse.

In 1734 the first lighthouse in Canada went into operation at Louisbourg. The 24-metre (70-foot) tower, gutted by fire in 1736, was rebuilt in 1738 and finally destroyed by the British in 1758.

One of the most picturesque spots on Grand Manan Island is the lighthouse, known as Swallowtail Light, at the top of a peninsula at North Head. A little patience may reward you with a view of whales, which regularly pass by just offshore.

Sable Island had two lighthouses, one at the western tip and one at the eastern tip. The western lighthouse, built in 1873, has been moved because of erosion in 1883, 1888, 1917, 1940 and 1951.

A device responsible for saving thousands of mariners' lives was invented by a Scot, Robert Foulis, who moved to Saint John. He presented his steam fog whistle to lighthouse commissioners in New Brunswick in 1853, and in 1860 the first steam foghorn in the world was installed on Partridge Island. Lighthouses had been used in the Maritimes since 1758 but had not always been effective in warning ships of danger, particularly in fog. Because noise travels farther in a pea-souper than does light, large bells were used by the mid-1800s, but the sound didn't always travel far enough. Something that could be heard from a great distance, and that could send out long and short blasts identifying the location of the lighthouse, was hailed as a major advance in marine safety, bringing recognition to its inventor. Some of his fog whistles are still in use.

OUT OF THE WOODS

The Maritimes pioneered the lumber business in North America with the first sawmill, a water-powered pit mill, erected in 1612 near Annapolis Royal. Because there were lots of rivers and streams to provide water power, sawmills began popping up all over the place. Also in Nova Scotia, at about the same time, Nicolas Denys built a residence and sawmill on the LaHave River and began shipping oak to France.

Lumber pioneers, such as the colourful "Main John" Glasier, worked the upper reaches of the St. John River valley, using brains and brawn to establish the wide river as a sluiceway for their logs. At Grand Falls, the river drops 23 metres and then narrows in a gorge about two kilometres long, where the tumultuous action of the water has worn deep holes, or wells, into the rocks. Sometimes logs would fall into a whirlpool where they would be whipped around and around upright, their ends ground to points, earning the whirlpool the name "The Coffeemill." The gorge has prompted the same kind of tales and stunts as Niagara Falls and is well worth a visit.

It has been estimated that the average amount of rum consumed in New Brunswick during the days of the great lumber camps equalled an amazing 20 gallons a year for every male worker over 16.

The first paper boxes made in Canada (Saint John), in 1878, were in big demand by shoemakers.

The first lumber, cut to build homes, furniture and ships, quickly depleted hardwood forests. Prince Edward Island, for example, was stripped to the point where only tiny stands of oak remain today. The lumber industry must have been relieved when the demand for softwood for papermaking came along. Pulp and paper demands have been the main market for regional forests for more than 100 years. At the rate the forests are being clear-cut, they won't last another 100 years, though there has been some replanting. In 1977 Irving Woodlands reached a milestone as K. C. Irving planted the 100 millionth seedling. Somehow the rows of seedlings planted in clear-cut land don't have the same appeal as our natural forests.

Today, New Brunswick has 2.5 percent of Canada's productive forest land but supplies 4.9 percent of the total harvest. Pulp and paper mills, lumber mills and furniture factories are the mainstays of the industry. The most plentiful trees are spruce and fir, favoured in the production of pulp and paper.

 The spars and masts of Admiral Nelson's fleet at the Battle of Trafalgar were made from white pine floated down the St. John River from the Republic of Madawaska.

And to think it all started with a teenager in Halifax. Young Charles Fenerty, it seems, had a fascination with wasps and came up with the idea of papermaking from wood when he watched them chew wood fibres to make their nests. He began experimenting in 1838, working with spruce pulp. In 1844 his firm white paper was apparently exhibited. Paper was certainly available before that time, but it was made primarily from rags and cloth. A rag papermill was established in Bedford Basin in 1819, but the mill couldn't get the cotton, linen or rags needed to make paper. All three were in short supply in Europe, causing great restrictions on the size of paper that could be produced until 1817 or 1818. Fenerty didn't patent his process. A German did. Fenerty got no recognition for his work, which became the founding point of the modern pulp and paper industry – Canada's biggest industry. Paper is our greatest export.

HOW WE GET AROUND

"The *Richard Smith* was the first vessel to enter Charlottetown harbour without the usual show of sail. People stood and gazed as we might today if we saw a rocket ship. The Indians of Point Prim regarded the "smoke-boat" with superstitious awe and the citizens thronged the wharf in wonderment. Little did they realize that soon a sooty cloud issuing from ten thousand funnels would stifle their graceful ocean birds, which, with snowy wings and body poised, skimmed the seven seas. The days of sail would pass and that ship, the *Richard Smith* of Pictou, marked the beginning of the end."

— George Edward Hart,
The Story of Old Abegweit, 1935

For carrying household goods or game over the snow, the Micmac made a sled with a turned-up front by splitting a thin slab from a rock maple tree. The word *toboggan* comes from the Micmac word for these sleds. They also made snowshoes.

Many of the earliest roads used log bridges over swamps and gullies. Laid close to one another, without the spaces between them filled, the logs were very rough, "Would jolt passengers to pieces" and were referred to as a disgrace in reports sent back to England as late as 1826. Because they resembled a famous cloth worn by a king, they were called corduroy roads.

In the 1820s, steamboats appeared, and a Halifax–Quebec run began. The *Royal William* made history in 1833 when it became the first steamship to cross the Atlantic under steam the whole trip. Nova Scotians, an aggressively seagoing lot, were quick to catch what this feat meant for the future. A movement was afoot to acquire financing in Britain and the United States for a fast mail-and-passenger service across the Atlantic. It was a risk that financiers hesitated to take.

Not young Samuel Cunard, though, born in Halifax in 1787. His United Empire Loyalist father, Abraham Cunard, was a worker at the Halifax dockyards. Samuel, a rising young businessman, was convinced that "steamers properly built and manned might start and arrive at their destination with the punctuality of railroad trains." In 1840 Samuel's *Britannia* inaugurated regularly scheduled steamship service between the two continents – the first of the "Cunarders" that were to girdle the world.

For nearly 150 years, through peace and war, ships belonging to the company founded by Samuel Cunard have played a major role in ocean transport. An advertising campaign claimed, "Getting there is half the fun."

Goin' Down The Road

Maritimers have a long tradition of leaving their native shores to seek work where it can be found – a fact of life known in these parts as "goin' down the road." On July 28, 1891, the first harvest excursion left for western Canada with 1,300 workers, the first of an annual stream of men, young and not so young, from all parts of Canada and England. Many Maritimers were lured by high wages – the highest ever paid to transient workers. Beginning at $1.50 a day, they jumped to $2 and then to $3.50 until 1915, when a huge bumper crop sent wages soaring to $6. Jumping aboard trains bound for the Canadian west was too much for our boys to pass up. The money earned would often be enough to feed a family for a whole winter. There was also an annual flow of lumbermen to the Maine woods.

These work patterns haven't changed much. Young people still set their sights on jobs in Ontario or Alberta. Just the trains are gone, and gone with them is the camaraderie of the harvest excursions. So important were these excursions that furloughs were granted to men of the Canadian Expeditionary Forces who were still in training camps in Canada preparing to do battle in 1915.

These days, most Maritimers want a share in modern, industrialized society, yet they want to avoid the harsher effects that it can have on communities. People here still live differently from those in other parts of Canada. There is still less emphasis on ownership of goods as a measure of one's worth and more on friends, family and community.

Maritimers value a pace of life that is a little slower, a little more relaxed, as do the many tourists who look upon our lifestyle with envy and can often be heard to say that visiting the Maritimes is like taking a step back to a better time.

CHAPTER 4

OUR WONDERFUL, FOOD & DRINK

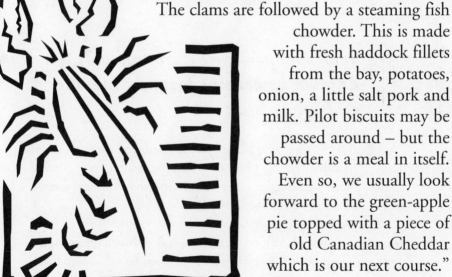

"We usually start with clams, which are steamed in sea-weed. To our family, it would be difficult to imagine any-thing more delicious as an *hors d'oeuvre* than these small clams eaten with melted butter and vinegar – about two dozen per person. The clams are followed by a steaming fish chowder. This is made with fresh haddock fillets from the bay, potatoes, onion, a little salt pork and milk. Pilot biscuits may be passed around – but the chowder is a meal in itself. Even so, we usually look forward to the green-apple pie topped with a piece of old Canadian Cheddar which is our next course."

– Dr. Charles Best, co-discoverer of insulin,
from a description of his favourite "shore meal"
at Passamaquoddy Bay, New Brunswick

89

Folks have always come to the Maritimes to eat. Today's tourists salivate over the same foods enjoyed centuries ago by our ancestors. The fact that we have been eating these foods for so long testifies to both their goodness and their integral place in the bounty of these provinces by the sea.

Nomadic Natives followed herds of "dinner on the hoof" – caribou. Primarily meat eaters, their diet included rabbit, bear, beaver, moose, porcupine and seal. They fished. They harvested oysters, mussels and clams. Strawberries, blueberries, raspberries, blackberries, tea berries and cranberries were eaten as they became ripe, crushed into a juice or dried and stored for winter use. Corn, squash and beans were cultivated. Tea came from the boiled twigs, bark and leaves of yellow birch, maple, spruce, hemlock and wild cherry. Nuts, roots and greens were foraged from field and forest.

In fact it was food that drew the first Europeans to our shores. Fishers, back as far as the Norse, followed the cod and came ashore to salt and dry their catch – the foundation of the East Coast fishing industry.

 Tourtière (pork pie) is traditionally served in Acadian homes on Christmas Eve after midnight mass.

Jacques Cartier, who landed on the northwest shore of Prince Edward Island on July 1, 1535, described the land as "very fair and so full of peas, gooseberries, other small fruits and corn that it seemed to have been sown and cultivated there."

Bannock, a simple, quick bread or scone made of four basic ingredients – flour, water, fat (drippings, lard or bacon grease) and a little salt – was cooked by early settlers on open fires. It is said that a similar dough was cooked on sticks by Natives.

The Micmacs helped the first settlers to adapt to new lands and introduced them to new foods such as maple syrup. The first formal agricultural settlements, by the French, were established to feed soldiers protecting their naval garrisons. The first European-style farming in North America took place in Port-Royal, with the first wheat for bread sown in 1606. The French settlers also built the first water-driven gristmill in North America, at Lequille, and counted among their number Dr. Louis Hébert, who might be called the continent's first horticulturalist.

For 100 years, Acadians prospered until the British ordered their expulsion. Some returned later, but their fertile land was lost, so they settled along the coasts. Isolated, and with less hospitable land, the adaptable Acadians learned to tap the rich resources of the sea. Old agricultural-based practices of food preparation were enhanced by new ones, which eventually developed into a unique culinary tradition still strong today.

Pâté au râpure, or "rappie pie," made with grated potatoes and chicken, clams or pork; *fricot* (a stew of potatoes with meat, chicken or seafood); *poutines rapées* (potato dumplings); cod and potato cakes; clam and potato pie; and many other fish and meat pies became Acadian mainstays, all with stick-to-your-ribs goodness. *Galettes* (oatmeal, molasses or sugar cookies), sugar pies and *poutines* (steamed or baked fruit puddings) satisfied those with a sweet tooth.

Other cultures were settling into life in the Maritimes. Elegant banquets hosted by the governors and their wives became the centre of British social life by the late 1700s, particularly in Halifax. The early 1800s brought waves of immigration. Scots brought their beloved oatcakes, scones and shortbread to Prince Edward Island, where they remain favourite fare, as they do in the highlands of Cape Breton. German immigrants in the Lunenburg area added sauerkraut, pudding, sausage, Solomon Gundy (pickled herring) and Dutch mess (salt cod and potatoes). Loyalists brought north the foodways of New England. The large number of blacks who arrived in Nova Scotia during the War of 1812 added their own cuisine.

In many ways, Maritimers of this era were better off than settlers in Upper Canada. Closer to direct shipping to and from Europe, the United States and the Caribbean Islands, they had access to citrus fruit, obtainable by the mid-1800s. Molasses had long been available; sugar cane gradually replaced it and home-produced maple sugar.

Onions were so prevalent in 18th-century Maritime diets that a Swedish traveller to Canada in the 1740s remarked that "the common people... may be smelled when one passes by them, on account of their frequent use of onions."

During and after the Great Wars of this century, an influx of war brides and refugees from Britain and Holland added to the rich cultural mix. They have been followed by immigrants from almost every part of the Earth. The result is obvious. Multicultural festivals are wonderful places to try dishes from around the world.

Nova Scotians eat more strawberries per capita than people anywhere else in North America.

Indeed, so diverse is our food that it is often difficult to get a feel for "Maritime" cuisine in a supermarket or restaurant. Country inns, small intimate restaurants, lobster suppers, wharfside canteens, community suppers, country and farmers' markets – these are the places to find the true flavour of the Maritimes.

DEDICATED TO GOOD CHEER

Samuel de Champlain realized that some of the problems of colonizing the New World could be solved by keeping the settlers in good cheer. He devised a plan that would alleviate depression and reduce scurvy. On November 14, 1606, at the beginning of the settlers' second winter at Port-Royal, Champlain founded *L'Ordre de Bon Temps* – literally "the Order of the Good Time," but usually translated as "the Order of Good Cheer."

Each day one member of the order served as chief steward or "grand master," assuming responsibility for the menu, which might include delicacies such as moose-meat pie, tender beaver tail, fresh salmon, roast caribou or breast of goose. The meal was preceded by a ceremonial procession in which members brought the festive platters to the rough-hewn tables. Thus, the Order of the Good Time – the first social club in the New World – fortified the spirits of those who created a new home in the uncharted wilderness and laid the foundation of a mighty nation.

Today the memory of the first members is honoured each time a new member joins the Order of the Good Time in Nova Scotia. Although the original order numbered only 15, distinctive membership certificates now adorn walls in almost every country in the world.

Good Food
For The Good Fathers

When the Fathers of Confederation gathered in Charlottetown to discuss the formation of the country, the city set out to entertain them with sumptuous feasts. Governor Dundas hosted most of the delegation at a dinner at which the riches of the sea were offered in prime condition and great profusion. At Government House, where the dinner was given, "the sea was washing gently up to the very door."

There couldn't have been a more elegant setting anywhere in British North America for the meeting of the men from the Canadas and the men from the Maritimes. Here they proposed and discussed and, for many hours of every day, laboured with the idea of creating a whole from the parts.

But when the parleying was over for the day, there were suppers and balls. Wives and daughters of Maritime men were caught up in a round of unprecedented gaiety. Middle-aged ministers, and a few much more than middle-aged, danced for hours and were fresh as daisies at three in the morning.

The Charlottetown Islander ecstatically reported the quality of the menus offered to the delegates: "substantials of beef rounds, splendid hams, salmon, lobster, salads, oysters prepared in every shape and style – all the different kinds of fowl which the season and the market could afford – all vegetable delicacies peculiar to the season, pastry in all forms, fruits in almost every variety – wines of the choicest vintage!"

QUEEN OF THE "KEEPERS"

Marie Nightingale has earned the distinction of becoming a house-hold name in the Maritimes; her name is synonymous with good food. A career dedicated to chronicling Nova Scotia's culinary best began with the publication of *Out of Old Nova Scotia Kitchens,* was followed by years as a widely read food writer and editor and continues with a succession of new cookbooks and articles. Now a grandmother, Marie has been shouldered with the responsibilities of matriarch of Nova Scotia cuisine and is acknowledged as a "keeper," just like her recipes.

"When I set up my first kitchen, changes were happening in the culinary world. I found myself caught in the metamorphosis that stretched between my grandmother's time and my own. The wonderful sameness of my grandmother's meals – roast chicken on Sundays, shepherd's pie on Mondays, fish on Fridays, baked beans on Saturdays – was a reflection of her era.

While my mother may have started out with much the same routine, the Great Depression quickly changed the menu. I remember being happy to have the hash, bannock and molasses Mother prepared for us kids, as she reserved the small piece of beefsteak or pork chop for my father.

Gradually, in the years leading up to World War II, meals were pretty much returning to the basics – meatloaf, liver and onions, fish, rabbit stew, baked beans – the whole wonderful works. Then the war, with its dreaded ration book, turned things around again.

It was after V-E Day that the major changes began. Now, we had casseroles. And Spam! Makers of this canned meat product switched their focus from supplying the army, navy and air force (the services had their own identities in those days) to wooing the consumer.

Food companies began hiring home economists to develop recipes that would create a demand for the com-

94

pany's products. The time of food fads had begun. While people with longer memories tried to dig in their heels, it was useless. Change would have its way."

— from Marie Nightingale's Favourite Recipes

HARVEST OF THE SEA

Fish, shellfish and crustaceans were an important part of the diet of early Natives, because they seldom lived far from the water. Eels and fish they speared through the ice. Weirs, traps made with long stakes driven into the bottom of rivers or bays, they used to catch fish. In fact, the Micmac taught Acadians weir fishing, a practice still in use today. Sturgeon were harpooned, salmon were speared and hooks of bone or copper were used for line fishing.

The waters off the Maritimes began yielding food for people thousands of miles away when the first European fishers ventured across the Atlantic Ocean chasing rich schools of cod. With no modern techniques of preservation, fishers would take their catch on shore to dry and salt before making the long and arduous sail back to Europe.

Cod cheeks, the "scallops" of the codfish, once tasted will never be passed up again.

When Tristram Halliday began canning salmon at Canada's first commercial cannery on the Bay of Fundy near Saint John in 1839, he set the wheels in motion to provide seafood for the global marketplace. Hundreds of small community canneries have been replaced by larger, modernized plants that freeze more seafood than they put into cans. Processing seafood has become a multi-million-dollar industry providing employment for thousands.

Visitors are so enamoured of our marvellous seafood that they want to take it home. Dozens of retail shops, especially near airports, will box up fresh lobster, scallops, smoked salmon, mussels, haddock, halibut, even swordfish or tuna. They will even deliver seafood to your hotel, packed ready to fly.

The demand for Atlantic salmon caught in New Brunswick rivers far exceeds the supply. Fortunately for us, fish farming in the Bay of Fundy is so successful that there is now salmon for all – at a very reasonable cost.

Nearer, my cod, to thee: Salt cod has been a Maritime export since the Norse arrived 10 centuries ago. Salt cod was light yet nourishing. In the early days, almost all of it was transported to Europe, but in modern times, when machine drying at inspected plants took over from wooden flakes or racks near the shore, new markets were developed in the Caribbean and farther afield. Contrary to reason, the driest cod is the least salted. In recent years, the industry has foundered due to the shortage of cod.

Cod was so important to the people of Louisbourg that even "throwaway" parts were put to good use. A local regulation stipulated that fishers set aside cod heads rather than throw them into the harbour for the crabs and gulls. The heads were collected by soldiers and the poor of the town for use in soups.

> The codfish lays ten thousand eggs,
> The homely hen lays one.
> The codfish never cackles
> To tell you when she's done.
> And so we scorn the codfish,
> While the humble hen we prize,
> Which only goes to show you
> It pays to advertise.
>
> *– anonymous*

After an overnight soaking and many changes of water, flaked salt cod can be creamed with peas or made into fish cakes, which remain a favourite in many rural homes. One recipe for "codcake" combines salt cod, potatoes, onion, eggs and bacon – a meal in a patty.

East Coast singer-cum-restaurateur Catherine MacKinnon features Nova Scotian fish cakes, made the old way with salt cod, on the menu at her new restaurant, Spot o' Tea, in Prince Edward Island. Food and music have become intertwined in MacKinnon's life. At the grand old age of eight, her first professional performance earned her a single jar of peanut butter in payment. Rita MacNeil, another of our musical treasures, also has a tearoom. Hers is in Cape Breton. She isn't known for her salt cod, but her tea and sandwiches are great!

The "sole" caught in waters off Nova Scotia is actually flounder. Whatever, it is delicious!

Of all the types of fish that Maritimers smoke, the snakelike eel is the most unusual. Born in the seaweed of the Sargasso Sea, far south in the North Atlantic, baby eels travel with the Gulf Stream. Some, the North American eels, stop here, whereas the European ones keep going. Caught in marshlands, eels are most commonly smoked, but they are also hung outside by a nail through the head, their skin peeled off like a sock from a foot and their flesh chunked and cooked in a skillet, where it jumps and snaps in the hot fat.

In *The Fascinating World of New Brunswick,* Stewart Trueman wrote about visiting a smokehouse at Seal Cove:

> "It was not a place to smoke, but a two-storey wooden building that continually seemed to be on fire, if you could believe the black fumes seeping through the cracks of the window-shutters and from under the high-raised open roof ridge. But that's the way it's supposed to be – great logs smothered in sawdust, smoulder and spark continuously on the ground floor, while the second-storey ceiling is literally frescoes with tens of thousands of salted herring hanging by their gills, slowly being smoked into a rich lustrous hue as if wrapped in iridescent golden tinsel."

There were once 300 smokehouses on Grand Manan Island alone. Mariners could find their way home by following the pall of smoke. Although the numbers have decreased, and stainless steel smokers have replaced most of the old houses, Maritime smoked salmon, mackerel, eel, trout, scallops, mussels, even lobster, grace the tables of the world.

Dark Harbour, on the cliff-girt western side of Grand Manan, is the world centre of the dulse-gathering industry. Sun dried, this seaweed can be eaten raw or toasted. The fact that it's high in iron, iodine and other good nutrients – not to mention its sweet taste – encourages some folks to sprinkle dulse on a salad or use it powdered to give a seacoast piquancy to casseroles and chowders.

For great lobster, cook it in seawater with a piece of seaweed.

Around the Bay of Fundy, you are as likely to see roadside signs offering "Dulse, Clams in the Shell, Lobster or Periwinkles" as you would be to see signs for strawberries, corn or fresh vegetables in other provinces.

Fisherman Ervin Myers and his wife, Ethelda, raised 13 daughters in a tiny shingle house with only the money he could get for fish and winter work in the woods. Like most rural families of the day, they knew how to take care of themselves. They raised and put down root crops, making mulches of seaweed, manure and compost to fertilize the soil. Near their orchard, they grew hops to use as yeast and cold medicine, and they harvested the sea, saving scarce cash for necessities such as tea. Their way of life typifies that of many inshore fishers. It was a subsistence economy, dependent on their ability to take advantage of the natural resources around them. This made them self-sufficient but never rich. They subsisted with what Jeddore Oyster Ponds could provide them. Their home is now a museum.

Oysters have had a reputation as an aphrodisiac for hundreds of years. Add the fact that they taste wonderful and it is no surprise to discover that they were extremely popular in the 18th century, with many a wild and wonderful all-male party featuring oysters and wine. The liking for oysters wasn't limited to the men, of course. In fact, a century before Louisbourg was founded, Nicholas Denys wrote that during the winter there was a "great mania" for oysters among the fishing population of Atlantic Canada. Chopping holes in the ice, the people would scoop oysters from the seabed and take them ashore to cook them over the coals of a fire, supplementing their meal with "water, crumbs of bread and a little pepper or nutmeg."

The old adage that you can only eat oysters in a month with an 'r' has gone by the wayside thanks to modern cold storage. The industry is also managed for year-round harvests and has reseeding and cultivation programs to ensure a constant supply.

Oysters tend to be named for the region from which they come. My favourite is the Malpeque, from Prince Edward Island. Once you savour the Malpeque's distinctive flavour, which a chef friend describes as "of the sea," you will know why it is so much in demand by connoisseurs.

"Because oysters are so readily available they are often eaten by Islanders as snacks. Tales abound of men sitting out back of the barn with a pail of oysters between their knees, just gossiping, shucking and slurping. From the way some of the oldtimers talk, it was common practice to down a pailfull each. Since they are said to be an aphrodisiac, I wonder if they are the indirect cause of so many large Island families."

– *from Favourite Recipes from Old Prince Edward Island*

Truth is that you haven't really had a Maritime experience until you've done two things.

One is clam digging. To find clams, look for small holes in the sandflats at low tide. Watch for a little squirt of water. If you see one, dig like crazy with a fork or shovel. Push straight down, then flip out the sand. About a foot down, you should luck into a clan of clams ready to pop into your bucket. Now the secret: collect clams several hours before you need them, then give them a last supper of corn meal served in a pail of saltwater. It will take away any grit as it speeds through the clam, making for a better feast. The ultimate clambake: steam the clams on a bed of fresh seaweed over a bonfire at the shore. We do the same with mussels. It's a reason to visit!

The other thing is eating a lobster from scratch, just like you would out on the boat. No crackers, no scissors, no tools. Just fingers, teeth and a will to enjoy the most succulent seafood you can imagine.

A Down~Home Lobster "Feed"

Chefs are always coming up with wonderful new ways to enjoy lobster, but the old way is still the most popular. I will never forget my first true lobster feed in Nova Scotia.

Dozens of lobsters were boiled in a cauldron of seawater over an outside fire. The table was covered in layers of newspaper, a chopping block and a big old knife in the middle. You have to use an old cleaver because the shell can chip the blade. There were small bowls, some with white vinegar, others with lemon juice and melted butter. On a sideboard were rolls, potato salad and pies for dessert.

Once the lobsters were cooked and drained, huge piles were dumped on the table. Ten of us sat down, and the feasting began. Notice that I didn't mention utensils or plates on the table. There were none. After a time, I was graciously presented with an old fork with bent tines to help get the meat out. The blunt handle is good for pushing through the meat in the segmented "knuckle" of the claw; the bent tines get into the "thumb" of the claw.

Here's how you do it. Grab the lobster in both hands, one at the head, one at the tail, making sure that none of the spines or sharp sticky-out bits will puncture your hand. Twist the lobster sideways, separating head from tail. Break the flipper bits off the tail, and then push your finger or the handle of a fork or knife into the small end of the tail. The tail meat should push right out. Look for the little flap at the lower end of the tail and peel it back the full length of the meat to expose the black vein. Pull or wash it out and you have a succulent chunk of meat ready to eat. Next rip off the legs, breaking them apart at the joints. There's meat in the tail flippers and legs as well; break them open, and then use your teeth to nibble it out. Twist the thumb off the claw, place the claw on the chopping block and whack it with a cleaver. With a little practice, you'll soon know just how hard to hit it to split the shell but not the meat underneath. True lobster lovers also delve into the body seeking out morsels of meat. The only part of the lobster not edible is the stomach, right up behind the eyes.

Morsels of meat can be dipped into the vinegar or lemon-butter mix or eaten au naturel.

Follow this method of eating with your hands and you can easily imagine sitting at a trestle table in days long past and enjoying a Tom Jones-style feast. Clean-up is easy too: put the shells into a pail, which can be dumped on the garden later, and roll up the mess in the newspapers. No fuss, no muss – just many sticky hands.

At the other end of the eating spectrum, chefs from Seasons in Thyme in Summerside, Prince Edward Island, have created a rich red lobster oil that, as well as being a flavour enhancer, is in demand for its use in plate decoration by top chefs.

Digby scallops are to die for: scrumptious white meat at its best when fried in a little butter and eaten hot. Best place to buy 'em? Down on the wharf in Digby – or, surprisingly, on the Via Rail overnight train to Montreal.

Lobster attain the greatest weight of any living arthropod, the largest on record weighing 19.1 Kg (42 pounds).

As common fish stocks dwindle and our marketplace expands, the Maritime fishing industry undergoes radical change. Periwinkles, bill fish, razor clams and starfish are exported. Sea urchins are prized in Asia for the delectable flavour of their ovaries and testes. Diners remove the succulent gonads for a dish that resembles caviar. This is a delicacy in Japan, and what was once a pest has become a $3.5 million business a year for Nova Scotia. Snow crabs in the 1960s were considered a "trash" species. In the late 1990s, they add another $30 million to Nova Scotia's economy alone. One enterprising fellow, Tom Reyno of Sambro, Nova Scotia, is even making dog snacks from dogfish.

THE NOBLE SPUD

You can't take a summer drive in Prince Edward Island without passing acre after acre of potatoes. In fact, the carefully tended fields, green rows against the rich red soil, are so picturesque they are one of the attractions marketed by the province.

The first record of potato production in Prince Edward Island comes from a 1771 report sent by the colonial governor to England describing the year's crop as a "phenomenal success." By 1790 island farmers were exporting small quantities of potatoes to Nova Scotia and New Brunswick; by 1830 they were sending potatoes to the West Indies. In fact, because of the nature of transportation and the poor quality of the roads, it was easier and cheaper for some farmers to ship potatoes to the West Indies via a local port than to get them to market in Charlottetown by road.

Potatoes became so central to the Maritime diet that they were often served at every meal. In early days, they frequently were the meal!

Potatoes continue to be a phenomenal success for the island and are its primary cash crop, with almost 620 farmers planting about 108,000 acres, with an average yield of 250 hundredweight per acre in the late 1990s. That's 26 million 100-pound bags, or 1,181,000 tonnes.

 The first known agricultural exhibition in North America, begun at Windsor, Nova Scotia, in 1765, continues today.

Varieties have changed over the years as the demand for seed, tablestock and processing potatoes has changed. The most popular potato on Prince Edward Island is the Russet Burbank, used to produce frozen french fries and as a baking potato. Others include Shepody, Kennebec, Superior, Yukon Gold, Goldrush, Century Russet and Chieftain. More than 30 varieties are grown to supply customers in North and South America, Europe, the Middle East and Africa.

The first certified disease-free seed potatoes developed in Canada, Irish Cobblers, were shipped from Prince Edward Island to Ontario in 1918. There is a great demand for Canadian certified seed potatoes in foreign countries. Potato growing is highly specialized in New Brunswick and Prince Edward Island, where growers produce about eight percent of the total Canadian acreage of certified seed.

The Elite Seed Farm, at Fox Island, produces the basic seed for all potato varieties on Prince Edward Island. This 525-acre farm uses state-of-the-art technology to produce the seed, originated from disease-free plantlets grown in tissue cultures. In the spring, plantlets are transplanted into greenhouses and screenhouses for growth in a protected environment. Progeny tubers from these plantlets become the first generation of field-grown potatoes the following season.

Potatoes had many uses in the kitchens of early settlers. Residue squeezed from grated pulp for dishes such as pâté á la râpure became the starch for the family laundry. Potatoes were used to soothe headaches and to make yeast for bread. Small pieces made good corks for bottles. As a food, potatoes had no peer. During long winter evenings, slices were often cooked (like marshmallows today) until brown over an open fire. Grated raw potatoes, salted and cooked on the griddle, became potato pancakes.

The village of O'Leary, Prince Edward Island, is dedicated to spuds. Not only does it have a large Russet Burbank, but it is also home to a museum devoted to the delicious tuber, the Prince Edward Island Potato Museum. O'Leary also hosts the annual PEI Potato Blossom Festival. That big Russet – it's 14 feet tall, seven feet around and not much good for french fries. Made of fibreglass and steel, it pays homage to Prince Edward Island's most important agri-cultural industry.

"Bud the Spud," words familiar to Islanders from the 1968 Stompin' Tom Connors song about a potato-hauling trucker who "keeps ripping the tar off the 401," children's books and other songs, appears to be getting folks in a bit of trouble. Producer W. P. Griffin had been using a character called "Bud the Spud" on potato sacks for about 10 years when he decided to trademark the phrase.

Bad move. American giant Anheuser-Busch, brewer of Budweiser beer, mashed the idea, saying that people might think the brewery endorsed Griffin's products. For gosh sakes!

One of the region's leading chefs is known far and wide for his mashed potatoes. His secret? Parsnips. Chef Stefan Czapalay, located in potato country in western Prince Edward Island, is often called upon to create dishes with many varieties for foreign buyers to try. He has more than 27 potato dishes in his repertoire and can serve seven-course meals with potatoes in every course.

THOSE MCCAIN BOYS

The vagaries of history are indeed strange. The potato lies close to the root of the famine that brought so many poor Irish to North America in the 18th century. It is also key to the wealth and success of McCain Foods, founded by descendants of a family who left County Down, Ireland, in the 1830s.

The McCains prospered in the new country, farming and entering business as opportunities came along. Patriarch Andrew McCain was a quiet man but shrewd according to his son Harrison: "My father was a potato merchant. His specialty was exporting potatoes… Cuba, Jamaica and other Caribbean points, then down into Venezuela, Uruguay, Argentina."

Andrew's sons established McCain Foods in 1956 in Florenceville and set about developing a process for freezing local New Brunswick potatoes and marketing them to the world. The drive of Harrison and his brother, Wallace, set apart what could have been just any potato company. When they started, the market for frozen food was small, partly because technology only allowed the flash freezing of a limited range of products, primarily vegetables. French fries in frozen form had enjoyed little commercial success in Canada.

Harrison recalls those early fries with a chuckle: "We had to ask a big price, I think it was about 18 cents a pound. Then we cut our margins and dropped the price to about 14 and a half cents." Even so, people resisted paying this amount because potatoes could be had for three or four cents a pound, and they just couldn't see that french fries were worth a lot more. The McCains had to promote the fact that, what with losses from peeling and cooking, home cooks would only get about one pound of fries from every four pounds of spuds. Once the process of adding value to potatoes was explained, and time devoted to cultivating the market, people were quite willing to pay for the product.

That first plant could handle 1,500 pounds of potatoes per hour and racked up sales of $152,678 in its first year of operation. Ten years later, the company operated the third largest vegetable business in the world. Today, the McCain Foods plant in Florenceville can handle 60,000 pounds of potatoes per hour and is just one arm of a corporate giant. The McCains have a dessert factory, three french fry factories, a pizza factory and a juice factory in Atlantic Canada alone. They've come a long way on the back of the lowly spud!

FRUITS OF OUR LABOUR

Nova Scotia's Annapolis Valley has long been synonymous with the choicest apples found anywhere. But others fruit crops from other parts of the Maritimes have an equally distinguished reputation.

One of the first horticulturalists in North America to hybridize apples and pears was Francis Peabody Sharp of Upper Woodstock, New Brunswick. He developed many varieties, including the Crimson Beauty, in the mid-1800s. He established one of the earliest family apple orchards as well as an experimental fruit nursery. For almost 100 years, virtually all grafted varieties of apple in New Brunswick came from nurseries that he had set up, and apples became an important export.

Prescott House Museum in Nova Scotia is saving many older varieties of apples in an orchard commemorating the work of Charles Prescott, who grew at least 27 varieties in the first half of the 1800s, including Ribston, Pippin, Northern Spy, Baldwin and Gravenstein.

For years staff have collected varieties for popular fall apple displays, so they know where to go for stock for the historic orchard. Two to three varieties will be grafted onto each apple tree.

"K ing" of the pumpkin patch, Howard Dill of Windsor, Nova Scotia, has taken the orange veggie to unimagined extremes. Dill began growing pumpkins in the late 1950s and created a new pumpkin variety, Dill's Atlantic Giant. He went on to win four consecutive world championships, and his seeds or their descendants have been responsible for virtually every world champion in the last two decades. Working with a farmer-restaurateur from New York State, Dill conceived a worldwide weigh-off in 1983. The World Pumpkin Confederation grew (just like those pumpkins) until more than 16 weigh-off sites, mostly in North America, were established. Official weigh-offs take place on the first Saturday in October. Mammoth pumpkins have topped 1,050 pounds on the scale. That's a lot of pies.

A BERRY GOOD CROP

There's something about our Maritime soil and climate that lends itself to exceptional berry-growing conditions.

S trawberries as we know them can be credited to explorer Jacques Cartier, who found the berry along the Atlantic and St. Lawrence coasts and took plants back to France, where the berry was named the Scarlet Strawberry of Canada, *Fragaria canadana*. Similar plants were found in Virginia and South America in the early 1600s. Later various strawberries were planted side by side, and it is believed that an accidental hybrid resulted and became the ancestor of the big, luscious berries we enjoy today.

The first known cultivation of strawberries was at Annapolis Royal, Nova Scotia, where a governor grew wild berries in his gardens from 1710 to 1750. The first strawberry-certification program in Canada was developed in 1955 in Kentville, Nova Scotia. Eight nurseries sold virus-free stock for the first time. By the mid-1980s, the crop yield exceeded five million litres.

Blueberries now rank as Nova Scotia's top fruit crop, displacing apples. Low-bush berries are smaller and are best in muffins They are harder to pick than high-bush berries.

Wild blueberries, which are cultivated, are pollinated by "rented" bees each spring. Beekeepers from Boo Boo's in Prince Edward Island market Blueberry Honey, as well as that from rental bees working crops such as sunflowers or buckwheat. No, blueberry honey isn't blue.

The Micmac called the strawberry the "red heart berry."

There are over 100 varieties of cranberry, four harvested in North America. It costs between $30,000 and $50,000 to build a cranberry bog, a worthwhile investment: a one-acre bog at full production has a market value of between $17,000 and $40,000 a year. Cranberries are high in fibre and vitamin C and are said to have other health benefits. They are a must with turkey dinners and in muffins.

Partridgeberries (also known as mountain cranberries, rock cranberries and lingonberries) are the fruit of a dwarf bush that survives in the barren lands of Nova Scotia. Shaped like blueberries, the dark-red berries are sour.

SEASONAL SATISFACTIONS

Maritimers mark the seasons with food. It's true! As the great food writer Judith Comfort once said, "In the Maritimes, ingredients appear in the natural order of things. When the smelts are running we eat smelts, when the apples are red we pick them."

Fiddleheads and rhubarb are harbingers of spring. The May opening of the lobster season in Prince Edward Island, Cape Breton and parts of New Brunswick is the real beginning of spring, even if most of us don't get our first big "scoff" until the high prices of the first few days settle. Mother's Day in Prince Edward Island could be called lobster feed day. Strawberries, raspberries and blueberries mark the passage of summer, whereas the harvest and storage of potatoes, turnips, cabbage and apples do the same for fall. Oysters and mussels are at their prime when harvested in winter by cutting holes in the ice and sending divers down after them. Make sure you ask for cultivated or farmed mussels – that way you get plump meat and no grit.

Vegetables, such as Belgian endive, are a winter harvest, and today we have fresh tomatoes grown right here – under glass – the year round.

We do, of course, preserve. One sure sign of the end of summer comes with the "pop" that the lids on jars of pickles or preserves make as a vacuum forms. But nothing is as good as fresh food, and we are fortunate to have a 12-month harvest of foods so wonderful that we export them around the globe.

Fiddleheads, tightly curled fronds of the ostrich fern, grow along New Brunswick's riverbanks. They look like the peg end of a violin – hence their name. Likened to artichokes or asparagus, they have been described as having "a taste of the north with the flavour of the river." Delicious steamed with a dollop of butter, in a soup, with the New Brunswick favourite poached salmon, pickled, marinated, baked, sauced or sauteed, fiddleheads have become a visual symbol of the province. Natives gathered the greens, which they considered important as a spring purge, a tonic and even an aphrodisiac with fertility powers. They held the fiddlehead in such high esteem that they decorated their possessions with its image, which was believed to ward off evil. Today they are shipped to the world's markets frozen as well as fresh.

A good picker can collect 22.5 kilos (50 pounds) of chanterelle a day.

A golden-fluted wild mushroom that grows in Maritime forests is valued more highly out of the country than in its native home. *Cantharellus cibarius,* or chanterelle, gathered one morning for

108

Helross Products of New Glasgow, are on sale in German markets the next evening. The chanterelle taste is unique – definitely wild and woodsy – reflecting its origin in spruce woods, where it grows in moss carpets where the sun just breaks through the trees.

To Market, To Market

Saint John has what is probably the most historically significant, and the most interesting, market in the region. City Market, built in 1876, dates back to a charter granted by King George III in 1785, giving it the oldest common-law market privilege in Canada. The shipbuilding skills of those who built the market, located just off King Square, can be seen in both the hand-hewn timbers and the glass roof, which resembles a boat hull. Although the fare at the market meets modern demands, the ambiance holds the magic of yesteryear. Among the special stalls is Pete's Frootique, where proprietor Pete Luckett has found greengrocer fame. Pete is known across Canada for his television spots, which allow him to rhapsodize about veggies and fruits. His empire is growing, and these days he is more likely to be found at his new stores in Bedford.

Down Home Good Food

Early Maritimers relied on just a few veggies to supplement their diet: turnips, cabbage, beans, corn, peas and onions. Cabbages were stored upside down in the field after picking. When one was needed, it was brought in from the snow and thawed. Peas, beans and corn were picked, left to ripen and placed in the attic to dry. Soups made with dried peas and baked beans are still popular.

Home cooks loved one-pot dishes that could simmer away or be quickly reheated. Made early in the day, they didn't spoil if someone was late coming in. The working day for fishers, foresters and farmers began early and ended late. Wives' lives were simplified by a hearty meal that could be put straight on the table.

The tradition continues. "Boiled dinner" is one such favourite: corned beef, smoked ham or salt fish simmered all day with winter-stored vegetables added a few hours before serving. These meals are not only delicious due to the flavouring of the broth, but the slow cooking also tenderizes less expensive meat or fish.

Ties with New England, always strong, became even closer as Maritimers sought work in the woods. So close that New Englanders and their northern neighbours both lay claim to having created baked beans as we know them today. Maybe it was the Loyalists who brought them north. Soaked overnight, the beans are cooked all day with molasses, bacon, onion and sometimes a modern addition, tomato.

New Brunswick's Miramichi region is famous for its beans, with bean-hole beans getting rave reviews. Woodsmen built a fire in a hole. When the coals were ready, a heavy pot, filled with beans and salt pork, was set in the hole, covered with dirt and left for hours. Supper (or breakfast) just had to be dug up and it was ready… as long as the woodsmen could remember where they had buried it.

Balmoral Grist Mill near Tatamagouche, Nova Scotia, in production since 1874, boasts a Scottish kiln in which the oats are toasted using maple wood as fuel. This wood gives the oats a flavour that guarantees the best Scottish oat cakes ever.

Speaking of oat cakes, in 1775 the ship *Elizabeth,* bound for New London, Prince Edward Island, foundered during a November storm. The crew and passengers made it to shore in lifeboats. On the third day, the winds dropped and the sea became calmer, allowing the men to go back on board for provisions. They found half a puncheon of rum, sides of bacon, feather beds, blankets and cordage. A cask of oatmeal was washed ashore, but the waves had knocked the head out and sand had washed in. The men were so hungry that they scooped out handfuls of raw oatmeal and stuffed it into their mouths. Women made oatmeal cakes and roasted them in the fire. One gave Thomas Curtis a piece of one of the cakes and a bit of pickled herring. Later he wrote in his journal, "This I thought was the Sweetest morsel I ever Ate in my life though the Outside was burnt black and the middle not half done."

When, in the early 1960s, the Roman Catholic rector of St. Ann's parish in Prince Edward Island decided that the church could use money raised through lobster suppers to pay off its debts, he began a tradition that has been carried on for more than 30 years.

Grunt, buckle and fool are traditional dishes made with blueberries.

At first, volunteers helped in the kitchen and supplied the rolls, pies and sweets. After the first year, Father Gallant was able to pay them $5 a night. Gradually, it became a full-time summer operation. Today all proceeds still go to the work of the parish. St. Ann's and other lobster suppers are part of the vacation experience for thousands each summer, with little change in the menu over the years: chowder, mussels, lobster or an alternative, coleslaw, potato salad, jellied salad, homemade rolls and traditional desserts.

PROVISIONERS TO THE WORLD

Since early days, the Maritimes has exported not just foods fresh and salted but also foods processed in a myriad of wondrous and inventive ways.

It is commonly thought that Annapolis Valley apples were the first Canadian fruit to be commercially exported, beginning about 1820. How did traders miss those easily stored cranberries for so many years?

The Truro Condensed Milk and Canning Company was the first dairy in Canada to produce condensed milk, under the Reindeer brand in 1883. It must have been good, because it won prizes at food fairs in Europe.

Dr. Archibald Huntsman, director of the Halifax Fisheries Experimental Station in the 1920s, developed frozen fish, which he called "ice fillets." By 1929 they were marketed throughout Canada, making Huntsman the first in North America to freeze food commercially. He also pioneered refrigeration and storage techniques for seafood.

"Snickerdoodles" often herald the Christmas season. They are cookies.

Animal crackers were introduced when a Saint John baking company obtained North American rights to the complicated production machinery. Founder Thomas Rankine was a biscuit pioneer, producing sea biscuits or "hard tack" in Canada's first biscuit factory in the 1820s. By 1875, Rankine's was the largest bakery in Canada.

> "Following the announcement in the Guardian last week of the arrival in good condition of the first car load of fresh clams ever shipped from the Maritime Provinces to Central Canada, word was received yesterday of the arrival in Toronto of another car from Summerside. This is an excellent beginning in the Provinces on a profitable basis, and proves beyond doubt that fresh shipments can be made to the Central Provinces."
>
> *– the Charlottetown Guardian,*
> *June 29, 1932*

Only in Canada you say… . Although no one can argue the popularity of coffee, sold in hundreds of specialty coffee shops in the region, tea must be recognized as our premier hot drink. J. E. Morse and Company are recognized as Canada's oldest tea merchants, but it was the T. H. Estabrooks Company that reigned as Canada's tea king. Estabrooks had the idea that a high-quality tea, consistent in taste and attractively packaged, would sell well. He named his mix of imported teas Red Rose and assured customers that

"Red Rose tea is good tea." By 1900 the Saint John company had an annual turnover of close to two million pounds of tea, earning it the distinction of being the largest tea company in Canada. Estabrooks brought the first tea bag machine into the country. He eventually sold out to British interests ... Pity!

Sweet Stuff

Thanks to the close links with the Caribbean and the southern United States, Maritimers have never lagged behind when it comes to having a sweet tooth. In fact, they get downright creative about new and delicious ways to satisfy sweet cravings.

The oldest fish company in Canada was established in Lunenburg in 1789 by John Zwicker.

Henry Mott began importing cheap sugar from the West Indies in the mid-1830s, when he formed the Dartmouth Chocolate Works. His son, John, produced the first chocolates in Canada in 1844 at John P. Mott and Company. John, it seems, had acquired the knowledge of chocolate making from the first American chocolate makers, the Walter Baker Company of Dorchester, Massachusetts. The family continued to feed their chocoholic tendencies when Mott's daughter married into the Baker family, garnering even more assistance from south of the border. The company operated until 1920.

Meanwhile, another chocolate firm, the Moirs Company, began operating in Halifax in 1873. Its boxed Pot of Gold chocolates became a Canadian bestseller. Now located in Dartmouth, the Moirs factory outlet offers chocolaty bargains to visitors.

It is, however, the Ganong family that shines the most in the Maritime candy world. No trip through St. Stephen, New Brunswick, would be complete without a stop at Ganong

Chocolatier, a re-creation of an old-fashioned store, for some of the finest chocolate in the world. If chocolate is your passion, then visit during the annual Chocolate Festival in August. You can take a factory tour and watch demonstrations of hand dipping.

Since 1873 the Ganong family and friends have put their hearts and souls into the chocolate confectioner's art. Special skills in making quality confectionery have been passed down for four generations. They began by making hand-dipped specialty chocolates and continue to do so. In fact, the Evangeline cream bar and nut milk bar, which were the first to appear on the market, are still produced.

Chocolatiers Mott and Ganong were also in the soap business.

The company gave the world the chocolate bar when Arthur Ganong went on a fishing trip in the summer of 1910. He and his head candy maker, chocolate lovers both, wanted to take some along, but they knew the heat would melt bagged candy. The duo decided to try putting four or five chocolates together and wrapping them in foil, thereby creating the first chocolate bar. The Ganongs also invented the all-day sucker and the "chicken bone," a delicious "inside-out" candy that has chocolate in the middle and a crunchy, cinnamon-flavoured, pink, hard-candy jacket outside.

The Ganongs have been described as being relentlessly energetic, with a zest for life that few can equal. Their love of sports and activity kept them fit – a good thing when you consider that Arthur was noted for his twice-daily trips through the factory, even at age 83. He would bound up the stairs two at a time, perhaps getting his energy from the three pounds of chocolate he is said to have consumed every day. And it never showed – he weighed a constant 150 pounds.

JUST DESSERTS

Grunt, cobbler and buckle, delicious puddings made from whatever fruit happens to be in season combined with a batter or biscuit dough, are most popularly made with blueberries. Blueberry grunt is cooked on the stovetop; spoonfuls of biscuit dough are dropped on the simmering berries, which are then covered and steamed. Crisp and Brown Betty combine crumbs of stale cake or bread or cookies with butter and sugar, mixed with fruit and baked in the oven. Rolypoly is made with biscuit dough sprinkled with cinnamon sugar and rolled around apple pieces, which are then baked.

Plum pudding, snow pudding, canary pudding, Dutch pudding, dowager's pudding, suet pudding, rice pudding, carrot pudding, orange pudding, even crumb pudding. The list goes on and on. They are poured into traditional moulds and steamed for hours.

Then there are cakes: tipsy, lightning, war, hot water, hot milk, economic pound, wacky woo, daffodil, one egg, good corn, wind – we even have a Cinderella cake. And pies, molasses, sugar, vinegar, raspberry velvet, peach foam, rhubarb. Just goes to show that Maritimers do like their "afters."

YOU EAT WHAT?

Hugger-in-buff, a.k.a. fish and scrunchions, Dutch mess or house bankin, is a dish in which you drench salt cod and potatoes with a sauce made with fried dice of fat salt pork, onions, vinegar and milk.

Atlantic sturgeon, a remnant from literally millions of years ago that lives to be 125 to 150 years old, has occasionally been caught near Annapolis Royal, Nova Scotia. Sturgeon have no skeleton, but they come equipped with heavy plates and a thick "hide." It's not a common fish, so it's hard to find recipes for sturgeon. Most suggest putting it into a stew, but chef-owner John Gartland of Newman's became known for a cold curried-sturgeon salad – a complementary fit of flavours that "just happened."

Links between Cape Breton and Newfoundland are strong. "Newfie steak," for example (bologna to the unknowing), is a staple on many a "Caper's" table. The wood chopper's breakfast of ham, bacon, bologna, sausage, pancakes, home fries, toast, three eggs, tea or coffee served at the Country Kitchen Restaurant in Port Hawkesbury, Nova Scotia, may make the cholesterol-fighting, fat-counting world shudder, but it's common fare for folks who earn their living at hard labour out in the elements.

"You must be real tired and hungry. I'll do the best I can for you in the way of tea, but I warn you not to expect anything but bread and butter and some cowcumbers," wrote Lucy Maud Montgomery in *Anne of Avonlea* in the early 1900s. Many years ago, cucumbers were called "cowcumbers" – probably because this was the English way of pronouncing the French word *concombre*.

Hodge podge, an annual treat when the first vegetables come in, combines cream and butter with fresh peas, tiny "thinning" carrots, green or yellow beans and, for the fortunate ones with their own potato mounds, thumbnail-size nuggets.

When Governor Duquesnel died at Louisbourg in 1744, an inventory of his possessions revealed among his foodstuffs luxury items such as truffles, capers, anchovies, smoked salmon, almonds and a wide variety of spices, evidence that the governor's cook, Monsieur Duval, prepared dishes fit for a gentleman of position and taste.

 The word chowder comes from the French word chaudiere, which means "large soup kettle."

Summer savory, a flavour cross between thyme and marjoram, is a common herb in the Maritimes. Patrick and Mona Ryan have been growing and marketing it in Newfoundland and Prince Edward Island for 25 years, producing a staggering 4,000 pounds of the kiln-dried herb each year. Traditionally used in poultry stuffing, it also adds flavour to vinegars, herb butters, bean dishes, soups, tea and even pan-fried hash browns. It's good in a potpourri as well. It is very popular in Europe, especially in the Mediterranean region.

ODD FACTS

Malpeque oysters are the only creatures known to science to have overcome cancer on their own. Virtually extinct in 1917 because of cancer, this PEI crustacean developed a resistance to the deadly disease and staged a comeback. This resistance led to extensive scientific study.

Wild rice is harvested from a few freshwater marshes in the same way as Native people's ancestors did it – by beating it into canoes using paddlelike flails.

Seaweed pie? Irish moss, a seaweed that looks a little like parsley, fetches good dollars when cleaned and dried. Carrageenin, a starchlike, noncaloric extract from Irish moss, is used as a stabilizer in foods and cosmetics, makes a lovely pudding similar to blancmange and is found in many items such as chocolate milk and ice cream. To give it a try, visit the Seaweed Pie Café in Miminegash, Prince Edward Island.

QUAFF ONE FOR ME

Much of Maritime history has been "under the influence of" alcohol: obtaining it, consuming it, producing it, and even praying against it. Overquaffing led to the temperance movement, prohibition, rum running and homemade brew. Today we enjoy a good tipple without going to extremes. Wineries are bringing accolades to the region, and breweries conjure up fine beer. We even bottle rum and schnapps and have some fine malt whisky ageing in Cape Breton.

Wine, spruce beer and cider were standard household drinks in 18th-century Louisbourg. Enormous quantities of rum were consumed in local cabarets. Coffee and chocolate were popular but expensive enough to be only an occasional treat for the well-to-do. Tea was difficult to obtain, expensive and not as popular.

Rum, distilled from molasses or fermented sugar cane, played an important role in developing our part of Canada. Rum and other liquor provided much of the operating revenue for the new settlements through import duties. At five pence per gallon, though, it was deemed a little too much for the market to bear, reducing the amount of liquor imported legally into the colony. In 1751 Joshua Mauger built the first known rum distillery in Canada on the Halifax waterfront. Mauger was no dummy: he located his distillery near the naval docks. Good place to sell grog, aye?

Another distillery, started in 1752 by John Fillis, meant that a good portion of rum consumed in the area was produced there. Another blow to the treasury of more than one province came with the advent of rum running. A move to stop the smuggling by reducing the tariff to three pence was successfully blocked by Mauger, who didn't want his lucrative business endangered.

> "The women are industrious housewives. They also make their own yeast, and make a kind of liquor, by boiling the branches of the spruce tree, to which they add molasses and cause it to ferment in the manner we do treacle beer in England."
>
> *– John Robinson & Thomas Ripsin,*
> *describing women's work in the Annapolis Valley in 1774.*

Artillery punch was a favourite at hotel receptions in Halifax. The one from the Nova Scotia Hotel consisted of strong clear tea, rye whisky, red wine, Jamaican rum, dry gin, brandy and Benedictine liqueur. A little orange and lemon juice, plus an ice ring with pineapple rings and maraschino cherries, kept it … ah, healthy?

 Halifax's Brewery Market is also housed in a historic building, the former Keith's Brewery, which operated at the site from the early 1800s to 1971.

The Nova Scotia Brewery started in 1817, and in 1820 it became Alexander Keith's. John and Susannah Oland started brewing commercially in 1867. Their history is intertwined and complex, but the highlights take us to beer found on the shelves today.

By the age of 26, Keith had learned the brewing business, emigrated from Scotland to Halifax and started his own brewery. The year was 1821. In the Acadian Recorder, he advertised his "long experience" and his intention to brew "Strong Ales, Porter, Ginger Wine, Table and Spruce Beer." He went on to become very successful in both business and politics, but he will always be remembered best for beer. Keith brewed his beer slowly, carefully, taking the time to get it right. That's why, when his granddaughter finally decided to sell the family business, she looked to a man who had the same dedication to brewing as her late grandfather. In 1928 John Oland took on responsibility for brewing Keith's India Pale Ale for the Maritimes. There are those who still like it a lot. For over 130 years, the Oland Brewery has stood for pride of craftsmanship.

The Moose is loose! Moosehead Breweries was born over 100 years ago from a single vat of beer brewed in a Dartmouth backyard. Today this family-owned business – Canada's oldest and only remaining major independent brewery, the third largest in the country – spans several continents and generates more than $100 million in annual sales.

It all began back in 1867, when Susannah Oland brewed a single vat of beer from family recipes in her backyard in the Turtle Grove district. The Oland family's brown October Ale proved so popular that Susannah and her husband, John James Dunn Oland, were encouraged by Captain Francis DeWitton, a family friend, to turn their hobby into a business. After several anxious years, the brewery, called the Army & Navy Brewery, prospered. But just a few years later, John was killed, leaving Susannah a widow with seven children dependent on the family brewing business. By 1877 her brewery, renamed S. Oland Sons & Company, was flourishing. Susannah remained active in the family business until her death in 1886, after which the Oland brewing legacy was carried on by her sons. Since that time, the strong, resilient and highly creative Olands have been able to keep the brewing tradition alive despite fires, takeover bids, prohibition, the Depression, two world wars and destruction in the 1917 Halifax explosion.

Moosehead Breweries Limited produces eight types of Moosehead beer, as well as Alpine, Ten-Penny Old Stock Ale, Clancy's Amber Ale and Molson Canadian (under license for the Maritimes).

Even in staid Prince Edward Island, at the turn of the century, "cordial" was a secret treat usually hidden away for special occasions. The potency of the homemade liqueur is hilariously demonstrated in the stage version of Lucy Maud Montgomery's *Anne of Green Gables* when Anne formally entertains her friend Diana Barry for the first time and gets the wrong drink from the cupboard. It is one of the best scenes in the show.

The hard stuff aside, rumour has it that people are once more illegally selling drinks in Prince Edward Island. There is a prevailing story that truckers taking fish to Ontario are returning loaded with canned pop for sale. The cans have been banned since the early 1980s.

"Swish barrels," used to store liquor, especially rum, have long been highly valued by home-based enthusiasts. Water left to sit in the barrel will, over time, take on the taste and the spirits of the original contents. A good barrel gives results for two to three swishes. Later they can be cut in half for great planters.

I spent one stint of my working life as the lifestyles editor of the Guardian newspaper. I had quite a surprise one day when the women of the local temperance union came in with reports of their activities – this was in the mid-1980s!

Temperance in a Tea Cup, an original musical, plays at Orwell Corner Historic Village in Prince Edward Island, poking gentle fun at the recent history of prohibition and temperance unions.

Anyone who thinks the illegal stuff is "of the past" should think again. "White lightning" and "moose milk" (or "mother's milk" in Prince Edward Island, presumably 'cause we don't have any moose) lure otherwise staid fellows "out back" for a nip at many a social gathering, especially during Yuletide.

Sceptics once thought it impossible to establish a modern wine culture in the Maritimes, but thanks to new winter-hardy grape varieties that ripen faster and, more important, a few dedicated individuals we now have several award-winning wineries, including Jost in Nova Scotia and Rossignol in Prince Edward Island. Wine makers succeed by seeking microclimates for grapes and by making fruit wines.

In the 1860s, Johann Ziegler was granted the right to distill grapes, cherries, plums, pears and apples by the grand duke of the province of Baden in Germany. The historical right, observed conscientiously by his descendants, has been carried on for generations. When the Werner Rosswog family emigrated to New Brunswick in 1983, they brought well-guarded family recipes and expertise passed down from their great-grandfather and now produce "a wealth of delicious spirits," as they put it. Selecting sun-ripened New Brunswick fruit, they ferment and carefully distill it in traditional copper stills. An array of spirits results: apple schnapps, fruit schnapps, maple liqueur and blueberry liqueur. They also bottle Canadian whisky and white rum... all down on the family farm!

Nestled against the hills of Mabou, Cape Breton, the Glenora Inn & Distillery appears to have been lifted from old Scotland and carefully set down beside a bubbling brook of pure water. The water is one of the reasons Glenora has been able to distill North America's only single-malt whisky. The company also bottles special-label Kenloch, Smuggler's Cove, Cape Breton Silver and Confederation Bridge rums. The whisky, ageing in oak barrels, will be ready for first tastings around the turn of the century. That will be one big party and a great welcome to the new millennium.

CHAPTER 5

HOW WE HAVE FUN

"I know a fellow in Waterford, never finished his house over there. We were over there every Saturday night – dancing. He never put the partitions in, left them all open. Trying to make room for the dance – give them floor space. It was like that awhile. The television came in, and then his wife  died and he got married again. And the other wife, she wanted a television by this time. That ended that. (What did he do about the partitions?) Oh, he had to finish them, had to finish the house up. (Didn't need the dance room anymore?) No."

– Johnny Wilmot,
as quoted in *Cape Breton's Magazine*

If there's one thing that Maritimers can do, it's have a good party. We like to socialize. We like music. We like having the whole darn family around. Result is get-togethers that can be labelled as house parties, ceilidhs, times, frolics, kitchen parties. Or they can be a card-play, a play, a picnic, a do – all depending on where you live.

Now a "time" is defined (by T. K. Pratt, who wrote the *Dictionary of Prince Edward Island English* and knows about such things) as a party or community gathering, especially in celebration of some occasion, such as a marriage, anniversary or graduation.

Doesn't really matter what we call it, truth is that some of the best moments in a Maritimer's life are informal gatherings of neighbours and friends. How it evolves depends on the people: some just "hang together and catch a video," whereas others follow tradition and pull out a fiddle to render some foot-stomping, down-home jigs and reels.

Granted, things have changed in this era of cable TV and satellite dishes. House parties and small gatherings are not as frequent, in spite of easier transportation. On the other hand, the music, song and storytelling – the cultural heart of our people — are reaching a far wider audience. The growing appreciation of the talent in the Maritimes is enabling more and more of our performers to be heard farther afield. We are taking the party to folks everywhere.

We also love to meet and greet our friends and neighbours, and often we attend organized events with just that intention. Hockey games, flea markets, the mall, the theatre – we love them all. And they offer the chance to catch up, to hear the news, the goings on. One of my great joys is living in a provincial capital where I can, on any given day, meet someone I know.

Rural folk have an ability to turn mundane tasks into community events, upholding the credo that many hands make light work. Work and play bring us together. We have all heard of barn raisings, building movings and such, but some of these joint efforts have been unique.

A scientific awareness of the need to cultivate and care for the land took hold of PEI farmers in the 1800s, inspiring the application of mussel mud to fields. This natural fertilizer was taken from decaying shellfish beds once the ice was thick enough to support the equipment needed to haul up the mud and transport it. Horses were used to dredge it from river bottoms in the winter; it was then sledded over the frozen ground to the fields. The annual mussel-mud

In 1927 the Halifax Curling Club won the first Canadian men's curling championship, held in Toronto.

excursion was often a community event. Old photographs and drawings show gatherings of farmers with teams of horses ready to get the mud. Imagine the good times and good feelings as everyone savoured the satisfaction of a task completed for the year by enjoying a supper prepared by the women as their menfolk toiled out on the ice.

The determination of Maritimers to help one another surfaces with heartwarming regularity. Volunteerism is strong – whether the cause is to help someone in need by holding a fund-raising dance, push a hospital bed over miles of highway to collect change for hospital equipment, or pull off a festival, sporting event, or music competition to raise funds for a worthy charity.

They Come From "Away"

Having fun is what our highly successful tourism industries are built on. So just what do visitors do to have fun? Our attractions include magnificent scenery, friendly people, and many water-related activities at lakes and seaside beaches. But the real allure is tied to the history, traditions and culture of the region. People come here to do the things that Maritimers do, or did, as part of daily life.

The interior of New Brunswick has long been renowned for its hunting and fishing. Sportsmen came to the province to fish in the days of the birchbark canoe. Although both activities are still big tourist draws, there is a swing toward enjoying rather than killing wildlife, toward watching whales instead of harpooning them. Cameras often replace guns now, and there are catch-and-release programs in the salmon fishery in the Miramichi River and others. People still camp – in fact, with the RV added to the campground mix, outdoor vacationing is growing by bounds. In New Brunswick there is even a campground just for motorcyclists who travel on big touring bikes, hauling miniature tent trailers behind them.

Genealogy is responsible for some of our success in tourism. Over the years, thousands of young people left in search of employment and adventure, and now their descendants flock back seeking their roots. Historical riches are preserved throughout the region, some in the splendour of Fortress Louisbourg, others with a simple park or a historic site and marker. We are deeply aware of our heritage and fortunately are taking steps to preserve as much of our past as we can.

Nova Scotia reigns when it comes to museums and historic preservation. It has 125 museums and an ever-growing list of heritage sites. At the Fisheries Museum at Lunenburg, a schooner, rum runner and dragger are open to the public during tourist season – what better way to appreciate the life of a seafarer than to explore his home away from home. At the Maritime Museum of the Atlantic in Halifax restored ships are also open to the public. The Alexander Graham Bell Museum in Baddeck will enthral those with a love of inventing and things airborne. Sherbrook Village depicts an era – 1860-80 – when the village was busy with lumbering, shipbuilding and gold mining. Ross Farm Museum in New Ross is a working farm depicting farm life in the 19th century. You can go down a coal mine or climb up a lighthouse tower.

New Brunswick has two fine major historic developments: King's Landing historic village on the Saint John River, and the Acadian village at Caraquet. There are also dozens of museums and historic sites.

Prince Edward Island also has many fine sites and museums, including an Acadian museum and pioneer village, a historic village at Orwell Corner (where you will come close to the entertainment of yesteryear) and even a potato museum.

Festivals & Frolics

It seems that almost every community in the Maritimes has some kind of festival, fair or special "days" during the course of a year. Many reflect the ethnic background of the people in a community. Others celebrate a harvest. Still others seem to take place just for the fun of it. Some are huge events; others are gatherings that attract a small but enthusiastic crowd. No matter the size, festivals are a lively place for folks to gather and celebrate the uniqueness that is the Maritimes.

Canada's first known balloon flight took place at Saint John in the Star of the East in 1840. Ballooning has remained a popular activity in the area, and today the Atlantic Balloon Fiesta is held annually in Sussex, with over 25 hot-air balloons launched twice daily. A magnificent sight to behold.

A bunch of our festivals are rated among the top-100 attractions in North America: Nova Scotia's Digby Scallop Days, Celtic Colours in Cape Breton and Halifax's Jazz Festival; Prince Edward Island's Festival of the Fathers, World Dance Festival, Celtic Festival in Summerside and Lucy Maud Montgomery Festival in Cavendish, New Brunswick's Festival-by-the-Sea in Saint John and the Chocolate Festival in nearby St. Stephen – utopia for chocoholics!

Prince Edward Island's Old Home Week in Charlottetown used to be just that – a time when folks away came home for a week-long party and reunion with friends. For years it's been the highlight of the harness racing season. The Lucy Maud Montgomery Festival brings Anne fans to Cavendish, whereas fiddle fans head to the Rollo Bay Fiddlers Festival and classical music fans to the Indian River Festival.

Sam Slick Days in Windsor, Nova Scotia, celebrate one of Thomas Chandler Haliburton's best-known fictional characters. The Black Power Rendezvous takes place at Bridgetown, and a children's festival is held at the Black Cultural Center in Westphal.

The Micmac have a number of special events, most of them open to the public, including the Glooscap Festival at Five Islands, Nova Scotia, and the Micmac Annual Pow Wow in Halifax.

For a chance to enjoy some fabulous and unusual food and entertainment, check out the multicultural festivals. There you will find fresh oysters, Solomon Gundy, lobster, maple syrup, apples and more exotic foods.

Bridgefest at Borden, Prince Edward Island, celebrates the world's longest continuous-span bridge, providing the only opportunity to walk (or run) across Northumberland Strait.

Historic events are celebrated, such as the Loyalist Garden Party at Shelburne, the Sacking of Annapolis Royal and the Festival of the Fathers in Charlottetown. We have Irish festivals, Scottish festivals and a Brayonne festival (the biggest Francophone festival east of Quebec). Still other festivals celebrate folk, jazz, blues and baroque music, buskers, film, fiddling and pipes. And we have festivals devoted to potatoes, peat moss, lobsters, Irish moss, trout, antique autos, crafts, oysters, mussels and apples. You name it, we celebrate it!

HOLIDAY TIMES

Is a holiday an excuse for a party, or is it the other way 'round? I'm not so sure.

A friendly custom of the early 1600s in New France was strengthened by the Scottish settlers of the mid-1700s, who had celebrated the same way in the old country. Everyone headed home for the paternal blessing on New Year's Day, thinking that this benediction brought good luck in coming ventures. One would first call on immediate family, and then those "must" or duty visits were paid to other relatives, friends and associates. All calls were spiced with a little frivolity, a little wine, a little flirting.

Today there is a strong tradition of going to the levees on New Year's Day. Dignitaries receive guests, usually offering a little refreshment and a lot of glad-handing. For many the levee presents an opportunity to shake the hand of a politician or public figure and, in many cases, to see inside a residence or building that is usually out of bounds. People all gussied up, it can be good fun.

One of the first celebrations to follow the new year marks the birthday of Robbie Burns. Celebrations take place anywhere there is the most tenuous link to things Scottish, but few places drum up as much pomp and pageantry as Halifax's Members of The Scots. The North British Society, founded in 1768, still turns out in record numbers to celebrate the anniversary of the birth of Scotland's national poet, renowned the world over for his use of dialect and humour. Bagpipes, toasts, sampling the haggis, family tartans, singing and dancing are all part of an evening that is highlighted by the recitation of Burns's address to the haggis, composed in 1786. The haggis enters in a procession that "guards it from attack" by suitably armed members of the society's kilted North British Highland Scout Troop.

For many years in the mid-1900s, the first Presbyterian Church of Pictou would attract thousands of viewers from near and far every Easter. Masses of flowers, some 3,000 blooms, decorated the front of the church, forming a huge cross over the pipe organ, an arch and a mass of white on the choir rails. The fragrance, it is said, was as magical to the senses as the visual beauty. The flowers, a gift from Eugene Outerridge of Bermuda to the minister, W. L. Young, continued to appear for many years, until the death of the donor.

Pioneer Acadians of Nova Scotia looked forward to the special réveillon served on their return from midnight mass at Christmas. Awaiting them was a *gâteau,* baked in the household's longest pan, of birds, rabbits, and pork under a rich pastry cover.

Digby chick (smoked herring) got its name because it once replaced chicken at Christmas dinner for impoverished early Digby settlers.

Parties Big & Small

Music, dancing and a wee drop have always played a large part in good times for folks in these parts. An anonymous resident of Halifax noted in 1760: "We have upwards of one hundred licensed houses and perhaps as many more which retail spiritous liquors without license; so that the business of one half of the town is to sell rum and the other half to drink it."

In the 1800s, Fredericton was said to come alive during the winter months, when the legislature was in session. The highlight of the season was a ball sponsored by the governor. The waltz, quadrille, lances and minuet were popular in 19th-century towns, but rural folks preferred the livelier dodging-six, strip-the-willow, clog, old barnyard eight (known as "the one to make the feet fly"), jigs and the step-dance known as the "chicken scratch."

It is a little-known fact that Confederation was first merrily sanctioned aboard the SS *Queen Victoria,* the floating campaign head-quarters for the Fathers of Confederation. Anchored in Charlottetown Harbour, the iron steamship played host to a jolly party on September 3, 1864, where the coming together to form a nation was unofficially proclaimed. The little ship played a great part in the official meetings that followed, collecting Maritime delegates for the Quebec conference and acting as a floating hotel for John A. Macdonald while "Canadian" delegates took side trips along the way.

Romance Is In The Air

The Maritimes are considered among the world's most romantic destinations by travellers from Away. From the beginning, it has never been far from our residents' minds as well.

William and Edward, sons of George III, known as the Halifax princes, left legacies that are with us today. Naval captain Wild William, a scandalous fellow, was best known for his after-dark activities (drinking, cockfighting and sleeping with John Wentworth's wife). His brother was his opposite, a military planner and church-goer, devoted to his French mistress. The fair Julie de St. Laurent was a commoner, so Edward could not marry her. Their years at their villa on Bedford Basin were idyllic. They could walk for miles along land-scaped paths that spelled her name. A heart-shaped pond symbolized their love. Prince's Lodge, a rotunda where musicians played for the lovers, can still be seen as you drive along the Bedford Highway.

Eventually, the princes had to go home, William to become king. He perpetuated the scandal of his affairs by making Wentworth governor of Nova Scotia as thanks for past "favours." Edward gave the city a clock tower, now a Citadel Hill landmark, as a parting gift. He became the Duke of Kent, and in 1814 he was obliged to marry a German princess and produce an heir, because William IV had failed to produce legitimate children. Edward's child was a girl, the future Queen Victoria. Poor Julie never recovered from the heartbreak of losing her lover and died in a Belgian con-vent.

Romance is often in the air at Silverbush, located in Park Corner, Prince Edward Island. The home where Lucy Maud Montgomery was married has become almost a shrine where many Japanese come to exchange their own marriage vows. It was at Silverbush that the author was happiest. She described the home of her Uncle John and Aunt Annie Campbell as "the wonder castle of my childhood." It is now operated as a museum by descendants of the Campbells, and they pay meticulous attention to duplicating as much as they can of the original ceremony for those who travel so far.

FASHIONABLY FASHIONABLE

"Corsets were invented by a cruel butcher as a pun-ishment for his wife. She was very loquacious…. He put stays on her to take away her breath and prevent her talking. This was inflicted by other heartless husbands. Ladies, in their defence, made a fashion to fit."

– Island Calendar of 1857

For many Maritime women, particularly in rural areas, fashions in the old days depended on Lebanese peddlers and their travelling "shops" offering clothing, needles, threads and, most important, ribbons, along with more mundane goods. The peddlers, incidentally, were also walking newspapers, carrying news and gossip from one home to the next. Many of these businesses evolved from horse-drawn inventories to shops – a general or corner store that often, along with the school and the church, became the core of a community – and clothing stores, particularly haberdasheries for men.

"Women's dress leaped out of the horse and buggy era. The peek-a-boo blouse was a beginning. Skirts became shorter and fuller with each passing year of the war until by 1918 they were swinging jauntily at the knees; but as a concession to modesty the legs were still partly covered by laced boots in soft leathers reaching the top of the calf. And now the lavish use of powder, rouge and lip paint, hitherto confined to ladies of the demi-monde, actresses, and society girls in search of publicity, became the preoccupation of every typist and shopgirl in the city and the world."

– *Thomas H. Raddall, in Halifax: Warden of the North*

Dorothea Stewart was one of the first 100 Red Cross Corps members to go overseas during World War II. She worked in London and then was sent to northwest Europe as a welfare officer at an ex-prisoner-of-war camp there. The Prince Edward Islander wrote about a "Wedding Dress" that arrived in London in a parcel addressed to "All Canadian Red Cross Girls on Overseas Service." The blush-pink wedding dress had been shown in a Simpson's fashion show but had never been purchased, perhaps because it was too flamboyant for the war period. Apparently, someone at Simpson's thought that the Red Cross workers were entitled to a little colour in their lives and sent them the dress. Delivery was slow due to a dock workers' strike, but eventually the dress arrived and was worn by 21 Canadian brides. The two-piece dress was in such demand that it was sometimes cleaned once a week (each bride paid for a cleaning). In the midst of a clothing shortage, the hem was raised and lowered, seams let in and out; with each alteration, another glowing bride exchanged her vows knowing that she look special – in keeping with the occasion.

Good Sports

We are a resourceful people, and if a way doesn't exist to have fun, we'll make one up. Our region lays claim to be the home of ice hockey. Basketball, invented by a Canadian, James Naismith, while working in Massachusetts, was first played in Canada in 1892 at St. Stephen, New Brunswick, brought there by one of his students, who taught at the YMCA. Other Canadian sporting firsts took place in this athletic part of the world.

The first Canadian four-oared rowing crew to win a world championship became known as the Paris Crew. The Saint John team made the headlines in 1867 by winning the World's Exposition international regatta, and they dominated the race until 1870, when they were defeated by England's Tyne Crew. A rematch was held in 1871 on the Kennebecasis River near Saint John. Our boys won, not knowing that the leader of the British team had collapsed at the oars. Spectators and press had gathered from both sides of the Atlantic for this great race. The river Renforth was named in honour of the British oarsman, who died the day after the race.

Bob Mills of Dartmouth won a bronze medal in rowing at the 1984 and 1988 Olympics.

Obed and Warren Smith, Caleb and John Nickerson and William Flemming (the spare) were, some said, the greatest four-oared rowing crew ever developed in Canada, even the finest in the world. All were fishermen and had practically been born with oars in their hands. Jerry Holland was their trainer. In 1876 they raced for the World Championship in Philadelphia and won handily, but the English crew cried foul. The referee awarded the prize to the English. Our lads refused to accept the $1,000 second-place prize. Apparently, the money is still sitting in a Philadelphia bank. They held, and still hold, the record for the three-mile race with a turn, 17 minutes, 58 seconds.

Rowing was very popular from the 1860s to the 1930s, and regattas attracted so many to Halifax that extra trains had to run. Haligonians eagerly followed the exploits of rowing heroes. In 1909, when John O'Neill raced for the North American Single Sculls Championship in Detroit, thousands met the train, carrying the champion home.

In 1920, the year before the *Bluenose* was built, Captain Thomas Himmelman was at the helm when the Lunenburg schooner *Delawana* raced against the Esperanto, the pride of Gloucester, Massachusetts, for the inaugural International Fisherman's Challenge Trophy. In 1997 his grandson, Hans, was at the helm of another *Delawana,* a custom-built C & C 44, which he guided to victory in his class at the Marblehead to Halifax Ocean Race. Thus, the tradition continues.

William Phillips of Saint John was the first Canadian to play major league baseball, beginning in 1879 with the Cleveland Indians. In 1935 Edna Lockhart Duncanson of Annapolis Valley became the first Canadian female professional baseball player, playing with the New York Bloomergirls.

Kent Walker of Charlottetown decided it was time to step up to the plate – in more ways than one. The island's chief umpire created *Hey, Blue!,* an international newsletter about umpires for umpires. The title refers to the nickname given to umps. Walker always loved baseball and became enamoured with umpiring the first time he tried it. Too old to work his way into the profession, he turned to the publication, which has thousands of subscribers and will eventually be a magazine. Who better to handle the extra demands of publishing than Ump Walker, who has a full-time career as a journalist and the ability to concentrate behind the plate on about 300 pitches every game?

In 1838 Prince Edward Island's Caledonian Club hosted the earliest Highland Games held in Canada. The oldest continuing Highland Games began in Antigonish in 1863.

Sports For When The Snow Flies

In a society where much of the work is seasonal, winter is a time of leisure. Fishers can't fish, farmers can't work their fields and related work – such as lobster canning or hauling produce – is not available. Maritimers take advantage of the good days for a little outdoor fun. Shinny keeps the younger set outside well after dark. Country ponds are cleared of snow for a Sunday skate. We ski and snowboard. We also have polar bear swims to welcome the New Year. And we park old cars on the ice and sell tickets on the day and time they'll disappear in the thaw – it's all part of winter fun.

You can't talk winter, or the Maritimes, without talking hockey. After all, we claim it as our creation, and most every male in the region, and a good many females, have played it, whether it's a game of shinny on a pond, a puck and a net on the road, or in the leagues in the local rink. Some of the fever has cooled, though. In the good old days, fan support was so strong that trainloads of fans would go to watch their team play. At times the fan support got out of hand, and the law actually banned fans from attending playoff games, especially during the era when the Maritime leagues were strong. Them were the days boyoh!

The first skating rink in Canada opened on January 3, 1863, in Halifax.

Canada's great game of hockey was first played in Windsor, Nova Scotia, about the year 1800 on Long Pond by the boys of King's College. This is the earliest known reference to a stick ball game played on ice in Canada. Hurley is an Irish field game that was adapted to the ice of Long Pond because winter made playing fields at King's College too rough. It then spread across the nation and became Canada's great winter game. Ice hockey is as Canadian as the maple leaf. Nova Scotia's newspapers chronicled the evolution of ice hockey from ice hurley between 1800 and 1850, and this chronicle designates Windsor as the birthplace of hockey – so says the Windsor Hockey Heritage Society.

 Summerside native Doug MacLean coached the Florida Panthers to the Stanley Cup finals in 1996.

James George Aylwin Creighton was born and educated in Halifax before moving to Montreal in 1873, where he taught new friends Nova Scotia's winter game. Montrealers loved hockey and began playing in 1875 using a wooden puck and sticks made by Micmac craftsmen and "Halifax Rules" laid down by Creighton. The game spread, reaching Winnipeg and Victoria by 1890.

Early pucks were cut from tree branches, replacing the leather-covered, cork-lined hurley ball, which was too bouncy for ice. Raymond Cope – and Micmac craftsmen before him – carved Canada's early hockey sticks.

Block skates were used when hockey began. They were replaced in 1865 by Starr Spring Skates, which sold for 75 cents a pair and became world famous. Starr's Acme Club Spring Skates, invented in Dartmouth by John Forbes, clamped securely to the soles and heels of boots and eliminated the need for leather straps and ropes as fastening devices. Made to fit any foot size simply by adjusting a spring mechanism, the skate was so much easier to use that it led to the popularity of the sport and ultimately to the construction of covered rinks.

In the early days of the game, rocks or metal posts served to mark the goal area. In 1899 the Nova Scotia Hockey Net was developed in Halifax. It caught on in Montreal and Toronto the following season, thus completing the basic equipment with which hockey is played.

Willie O'Ree, from Fredericton, became the first black to play in the NHL when he signed with the Boston Bruins. He and Truro, Nova Scotia, player Stan Maxwell became good friends. Maxwell signed a contract with Punch Imlach to play with the Quebec Aces of the Quebec Hockey League for $3,000 a season. As high-profile black athletes, they commanded considerable media attention wherever they played, although the good treatment did not extend to the ice. They were spit upon and subjected to constant name calling. But most frustrating was the racism in communities where they played, particularly in the United States. Maxwell recalled Imlach urging him and O'Ree to play like gentlemen as much as possible so that other minority players would get a chance to make a mark. There are still only a handful of blacks in the NHL.

Three brothers in Pleasant Valley, Prince Edward Island, invented a hockey tree designed to dry equipment after games and, more important according to the boys' mom, to keep the players' gear organized. The boys – Chad 10, Mitchell 15 and Nicholas 18 – are marketing their invention through Maritime stores, including Canadian Tire. It all started when their dad suggested Mitchell try building something useful while practising welding.

New Brunswick's Stacy Wilson was captain of the Canadian women's hockey team in 1998.

"Skiing seems to be coming in around Pictou. On hills in west end and east end young people are endeavouring to develop skill, and taking many a tumble in the course of the lessons... Down Carroll's Lane they go like birds, sailing across Water Street in front of sleighs and people. Tobogganing is also coming in and here again the small boy forges to the fore. We watched two toboggan loads of them spill themselves all over the foot of Deacon's Hill the other night. You wouldn't think there would have been a sound limb left, but up they got and at it again."
– *Pictou Advocate, February 9, 1923*

Speed skating was to Saint John what hockey was to Windsor. James Whelphey developed the Long Reacher Skate at Long Reach, New Brunswick. Ideal for skating on lakes and ponds with long stretches of ice, they were a forerunner to the racing skates of today. The skate is credited with increasing the number of marathon or distance-skating events worldwide. A challenge race from Saint John to Fredericton and back, and world-champion New Brunswick speed skaters and records, resulted. The inventor clocked 117 miles in 10 hours. Saint John became the capital of marathon skating and the home of the first indoor speed skating competition.

Raymond Smith, talking about smelt fishing on the North River Ice in Cape Breton in *Cape Breton's Magazine* a decade or so ago noted: "It's good fun, and it's good sport in it, too, when you go out like this — sitting in here nice and warm [in the fish shack], and then you go out and get 2 or 3 hundred pounds of smelts, like that. Then tomorrow, go over to Goldman's with them, and he'll pay you right there for them. And stop in the tavern coming home, and have steak and a beer."

These fellows get their smelt with nets. In Prince Edward Island, the sport is to spear 'em. Little communities of smelt shacks arise on the ice as soon as it will support the weight. Then the smelt fishers head out to their shacks at every opportunity. There is a certain sense of adventure – or something – in sitting on a crate in your shack, hot coffee (or cold beer) in one hand, spear in the other, leaning over a hole in the ice, ready to spear the first hapless little fishy that swims below. Tools of the trade include a sieve to scoop ice crystals out of the water and a bag to take the catch home in.

CHAMPIONS ALL

It must be said that Maritimers do not just play sports – they excel at them!

George "Little Chocolate" Dixon, the reigning featherweight boxing champion from 1892 to 1897 and from 1898 to 1900, and the bantamweight champion in 1890-91, was the most famous black athlete in the world at the time, earning an estimated $250,000 during his career. Born in Africville, Nova Scotia, in 1870, he paved the way for other black boxers. Not only was he the first black man to win a world boxing title, but he was also the first man to win a world title in two weight classes and to lose and then regain a title. Dixon is credited with causing a major break in the walls of racism and with doing a great deal for the self-image of blacks.

Nova Scotian Dr. R. J. MacDonald, at the time working as a lineman, trained as a long-distance runner in the evenings after a hard day climbing the poles. It paid off: he ran the mile in 4:37 in 1896, won the U.S. cross-country championship, won the Boston Marathon in 1898 and was comfortably in the lead of the Paris Exposition in 1900 when two local cheats passed him in a cab and took first and second place. MacDonald ran in every part of the United States and in much of Canada, bringing home 135 trophies. And, all the time he was running, he was getting an education as a medical doctor. He eventually retired from the track to practise medicine, first in Newfoundland, then in Antigonish.

Johnny Miles hopped a train in Sydney Mines, Cape Breton, in 1926 bound for Boston. He became the first Canadian to win the Boston Marathon on its new course, lengthened to Olympic standards. He won again in 1929.

Trenton, Nova Scotia, native Kenneth H. Doucette holds the record for the marathon in Prince Edward Island and is a Canadian Forces Marathon and Nova Scotia Marathon record holder. He competed in a 50-mile ultramarathon, 31 full marathons, numerous half marathons and five-, eight- and 10-kilometre races. When he ran his best marathon time of 2:24 to set the Nova Scotia record, he broke the record previously set by the great Johnny Miles in Boston in 1926.

Just after Johnny Miles set his record at the Boston Marathon, he went to Westville, Nova Scotia, to race before about 10,000 people. A young coal miner, Jimmy Hawboldt, raced against Miles. He had worked a 10-hour shift in the mine, walked about a mile to get out of the mine, then walked home for a bite to eat. He didn't have time to sleep, so he went straight to the race – and won it.

A bas-relief plaque in Saint John's King Square commemorates the seven world records set by speed skating champion Charles I. Gorman during the 1920s. All this from a man who had doctors dig shrapnel out of one leg from a World War I injury!

Motorcycle racer Don Munroe of Bedford, Nova Scotia, was the first racer in Canada to win the superbike, open sportbike and 600 sportbike crowns since 1989, when they went to a British Columbian. Kawasaki invited Munroe to join other international champions in Barcelona to test the new 600 ZX6 motorcycle – Munroe was the only Canadian to be so honoured.

Lori Kane's 1997 golf earnings of over $425,000 US established her as the best female Canadian golfer in history and earned her the title of Canada's 1997 female athlete of the year. And Kane was a rookie on the tour! She tied for first place in regulation play in the LPGA tour championship played in Las Vegas, dropping to second after three playoff holes. That win placed her 11th in earnings among female golfers in North America.

After all these years, Prince Edward Island finally has a gold-medal Olympian to boast about. Dave (Eli) MacEachern won gold as the brakeman in the two-man bobsled event at the 1998 Winter Olympics in Nagano, Japan. He credits his "general stubbornness" and his natural ability to push a sled for his win. Islanders are doubly proud because he's a genuine nice guy who quickly became a darling of the media. He plans to move from brakeman to driver for the next Olympics. Go Eli!

Upwardly mobile: Sharon Wood, born in Halifax in 1957, chose the unlikely occupation of professional climber and moun-taineering instructor. On May 20, 1986, two days after her 29th birthday, she became the first North American woman to reach the summit of Mount Everest, two months after beginning the climb. Called Everest Light because the group had fewer people, less money, fewer supplies and porters than an earlier Canadian team, they chose a steeper but safer climb up the Chinese side of the mountain.

They spent the first seven weeks establishing camps along the route, with the sixth about 2,000 feet below the summit. The stren-uous nature of the work exhausted all but four or five of the 12 climbers. It was decided that Wood and Dwayne Congdon, of Alberta, would make a first attempt and the others a second if possible. They left base camp on May 14.

After facing winds up to 80 kilometres per hour, and slowly ascending steep faces of ice and snow, they reached the summit of 29,028 feet. Wood was almost 20 percent lighter than normal because of calories burned during the climb. They spent about 20 minutes at the top before having to head down because the sun was setting. Such a long way to go for such a short visit! Because of exhaustion, they did not attempt a second climb.

Horsing around: Maritimers' love for horses has led to protection for the horses of Sable Island and for the Newfoundland pony. Thousands of Maritimers ride Western or English style for pleasure and in the show ring. There is nothing more pleasurable than a long sleigh ride down a country road with a daydream for company and time to savour the crisp air bearing the scents of winter: pine, wood smoke, damp earth.

Horses were an integral part of development in the Maritimes as well. The Nova Scotia Lumber Company, a thriving business in Walton in the early 1900s, kept 100 horses in the woods all winter, farming them out in the summer. The horses were transported to their summer homes by riding, herding and leading, even onto ferries.

When the "horseless carriage" first appeared, Prince Edward Islanders were not sure at first that they wanted to give up their horses and buggies for automobiles. There was a mounting concern about the harmful effects on roads and farm animals, a concern that stemmed in part from a general distrust of anything newfangled. As a result, the legislature banned autos from all island roads. The prohibition was lifted in 1913, allowing cars to travel every day except Sundays and market days. It was repealed in 1918.

Many Maritimers take to the sulky of harness racing – winter or summer – for the sheer pleasure of it. Horse racing even occurs on the ice. In Pictou, Nova Scotia, trotters and pacers were put through their paces on a track cleared from Market Wharf toward Abercrombie, with the challenge sent out to horse racers in New Glasgow, Thorburn, River John and elsewhere to take part in the fun. Ice racing still goes on and, when conditions are right, can be seen from the North River Causeway in Prince Edward Island.

During Charlottetown's Winter Carnival, streets are cleared and snow laid down for thundering races held right downtown on the main street. There is something magical about seeing trotters and pacers going through their training regime on a frosty morning. Snorting out little clouds of breath, feet fairly flying, horses race around the track or down the side of the road.

Joe O'Brien, harness racing legend from Alberton, Prince Edward Island, has been honoured with a museum in his name near his hometown. One of the most successful sports figures to come out of Prince Edward Island, Joe is a member of the U.S. Trotters Hall of Fame and a winner of over 3,000 races. He trained and raced standardbreds during a career that spanned five decades. *Gentleman Joe: The Story of Harness Driver Joe O'Brien* was published in California and is now being revised to add the last dozen years of his life as a successful breeder and trainer in California.

Harness racing superstar Mike Hennessey was born and raised in Charlottetown, then moved to Saint John 24 years ago. The 1997 season saw him win just under $4.3 million, which pushed him to $24 million in his career.

Back in 1932, Pictou sidewalks were plowed by a "very gentle red Percheron named Fred," who pulled a box-shaped wooden plow pointed at the front. The driver stood in the box as the horse plunged through the snowbanks.

"An eighth-grade dropout, an undersized teenager working as a lumberjack, a disillusioned 18 year old looking for work in strike-torn Toronto, he was hardly a candidate for fame. In Toronto he picked worms on a golf course in the middle of the night for a bait company. He was broke, economically and emotionally, and about ready to head back to a pedestrian life in Grand Falls, N.B., when a single question took him on another path: Have you ever thought of being a jockey?"

Ron Turcotte, the jockey who rode Secretariat to a stunning Triple Crown victory, was one of the most successful in the history of horse racing. *The Will to Win,* a heartwarming book by Bill Heller, chronicles Turcotte's remarkable story from his early years growing up in a large family of loggers in rural New Brunswick, his casual entrance into horse racing, his rise to the top and his life after a fall. Five years after his amazing triumph on Secretariat, the first horse in 25 years to win the prestigious Triple Crown, a racing accident left Turcotte paralyzed from the waist down.

Turcotte rode many of the finest horses of his time, including Northern Dancer, Canada's most famous racehorse. Under his whip hand, Secretariat won the Belmont Stakes by 31 lengths, a performance that defied logic. This was the world-record equivalent to 10 lengths faster than any other Belmont winner in 100 years.

In his racing career, Turcotte earned $29,606,205 and remains a popular hero in his hometown of Grand Falls.

GAMES WE PLAY

Games keep us sane in winter, be it cards, bingo, crokinole or one of many others. Before the era of television, families would gather around the kitchen table and play games. One family told me they had to buy a deck of cards several times a year because they wore them out so fast. Community halls, church basements – any place large enough to hold a few tables rings with laughter and buzzes with conversation as people use games as an excuse to get together.

Crokinole, a member of the shuffleboard family of games, is avidly played in the Maritimes. Crokinole boards often become prized heirlooms; they deserve a prominent place in the home and are often hung on the wall. Noted M. B. Ross, circa 1885, about crokinole: "A new and intensely interesting game for everybody, with no objectionable features whatever. There is no game where the element of chance is smaller, as the winning of the game depends wholly upon the skill of the player."

The Micmac have made and played waltes, a dice game, since at least 1600. Six dice made from the shin of a moose are tossed from a bowl carved from birch or maple burl. Sticks are used to keep score.

Quoits, popular in the early 1900s, was similar to horseshoe pitching. The object of the game was to throw a metal ring weighing about five pounds and have it land over a steel rod set in the ground. The Pictou County Sports Hall of Fame has a bunch of quoits memorabilia – that's 'cause many champions came from the area.

Sydney, Nova Scotia, was rich in Lebanese culture thanks to the coal mines that offered jobs. Tarbish, or tarabish, a card game similar to bridge, became popular among older generations of many ethnic origins. Its popularity spread to Antigonish and Halifax, apparently carried there by students.

John LaVoie has a fascination for dinosaurs that he wants to share, so he volunteered to teach grade 3 students all about them. To make the learning more fun, he invented a board game, PAN-GEE-AH, the phonetic spelling for pangaea, a Greek word meaning "all earth," in reference to the one big continent that geophysicists now conjecture preceded our modern continents. Designed and produced in Nova Scotia, the game is sold across North America. The object is to collect dinosaur cards and drive your opponents to extinction.

Our People Do The Darnedest Things

"A country's worth is not according to the number of square miles it possesses, but according to the square people it contains. Nova Scotia is very happy in this regard."

– E. N. Rhodes, former premier of Nova Scotia

Some Maritimers get up to the oddest activities in their spare time. Or maybe they think the same about those who don't?

Up to a dozen members of the Atlantic Canada Military Vehicles Association regularly squeeze into Bob McWilliams's dimly lit garage in Truro to try to restore a World War II-vintage Bren carrier to field condition. The Bren was used as a multipurpose vehicle during World War II and the Korean War. Once the tanklike vehicle is up and running, the group will take its treasure to car shows and parades. What's next? Well, they've heard there's a Sherman tank for sale.

Prince Edward Island's Archie Johnston helped his dad, Lieutenant-Colonel E. W. Johnston, build castles for a hobby. So many people kept showing up to see the miniature replicas of famous British castles that the senior Johnston was forced to open a tourist display. He figured that he may as well charge the visitors to help cover the cost of cleaning up after them and to keep the building fund healthy. Woodleigh Replicas became one of Prince Edward Island's most loved tourist attractions. Now 73, he recently winged his way to Ottawa to take up duties as a senator.

Photographer Sherman Hines has a thing for outhouses. Not only did he publish a popular book of photographs of some of our best outhouses, but he also produces a newsletter on the subject that has subscribers all over the world. He is even collecting some unique specimens for an outhouse museum.

Debbie Gamble Arsenault has 793 model horses in the room above her den. She is part of a worldwide network of horse lovers who display their trusty steeds (sometimes using photographs and occasionally "live") at shows styled after those for real horses. Models range from two inches to eight inches in height and are usually moulded plastic. This enthusiast makes and sells tiny bridles, halters and saddles and produces a magazine on the subject. "I love horses," says Debbie. "This keeps a lot of people who can't actually own a horse involved ... and you don't have to shovel after them!"

Coin collectors are a little miffed at the Royal Canadian Mint. In 1997 visits to seaports by the replica of John Cabot's ship, the *Matthew*, celebrated the 500th anniversary of the momentous voyage that Cabot and his crew made from Bristol, England, to what is now Canada's east coast. This anniversary was a big deal in Atlantic Canada. In recognition, the mint produced a commemorative dime featuring the *Matthew* in place of the *Bluenose*. However, most Canadians will never see, let alone own, one. Only 50,000 of the proof coins were minted, not enough for every coin collector in Canada. The Cabot dime is already selling well above its face value.

LOVABLE ECCENTRICS

New Brunswick author Ann Brennan heard tales about the legendary Klondike Kate from people living in Johnville, New Brunswick, and was so fascinated that she began research that would take her across the country and back as she pieced together the dramatic life of this adventurous woman. Now Klondike Kate gained a reputation as a boisterous dance hall queen during the Yukon gold rush. Truth was that Klondike Kate was a young woman by the name of Katherine Ryan who grew up in the small Irish community of Johnsville and in 1898 went off seeking adventure. She participated in the gold rush, encountering all manner of gold diggers. She was the first female member of the North West Mounted Police. She was one of the first women to walk into the North over the rugged Stikine Trail. And she was an early suffragette who became an important political figure in the North. The dance hall label occurred when a teenage opportunist from Seattle heard about Kate's exploits and adopted the name, along with the respect it garnered, as her own.

 Frog-watchers in Nova Scotia greet spring by counting and observing frogs, affectionately called "peepers."

One of our fellows became known as the Klondike King. Alexander MacDonald, a farm boy from Ashdale, Nova Scotia, headed west in search of fame and adventure, first to Butte, Montana, and then to the Klondike. He arrived in the Yukon in 1886 physically well equipped, and he used his size and muscular power well. After 10 days of panning with a partner, Big Alex, a.k.a. "The Bull Moose of Antigonish," had $20,000, which he used to acquire more leases and businesses. At the end of his 10th year in the Klondike, he was offered $11 million for his holdings by an English syndicate. He replied, "$30 million or nothing."

Big Alex adored gold for the power and influence it brought him, but the gold itself he disdained, once handing a bucket of nuggets to Lady Minto and saying, "Take it. It is trash." His charities were equal to his bulk. He built a Catholic church and funded half of Dawson's first hospital. He was presented to Queen Victoria and the pope, who made him Knight of St. Gregory.

Unfortunately, his fortunes turned. The massive man with the handlebar moustache had made bad investments and worse friends. He gambled. Fires destroyed several of his buildings. Penniless and alone in 1919, Big Alex was splitting wood in frigid weather outside his cabin at Clearwater Creek, Yukon, when he had a heart attack.

One of the most colourful Canadians — Dr. Edward Randolph "Painless" Parker, "extractionist extraordinary," and one-time carnival tooth yanker – became the world's most flamboyant dentist, building a chain of dental parlours in the United States and Canada in the early 1900s. The New Brunswick native funded his enterprise through spectacular publicity stunts: tightrope walkers from skyscraper to skyscraper in New York City, marching bands, elephants, publicly pulling aching teeth of lions and tigers, and gold-filling the tusks of walruses.

Another New Brunswick character was an impudent chap by the name of Henry More Smith. Innocent of face and full of fun, he achieved legendary status through his antics. He stole law books from the chief justice and then claimed a reward when he returned them. It is said that he even joined manhunts searching – you guessed it – for him and would proclaim that the thief was not far away! His career of crime took a more serious turn when he added theft of horses to his rap sheet. He was caught and thrown in the Kingston jail in 1812. It was not to his liking, so Henry faked an illness that had local women, and even his jailers, rushing to his bedside to comfort him. He used the opportunity to vanish. Today Henry could have found a career on stage: he could escape from handcuffs, open jail doors and twist iron bars. His charismatic charm eventually saved his neck. When sentenced to hang for horse stealing, he was given a pardon conditional on his leaving New Brunswick.

 Thomas Wilby left Halifax on August 17, 1912, in a Reo Special to become the first person to drive across Canada. He arrived in Victoria 52 days later.

I n 1917 Miriam Ruth MacRae Bird returned to her home in Cape Breton from California. She had married a Californian by the name of Marshall. He and another couple had made a bet with the Ford Company that they wouldn't go inside a hotel during the trip to Cape Breton. If they didn't, they got a new car when they got back. They didn't, and they did. They travelled 16,637 kilometres (10,398 miles) in cars filled with fruit so that they wouldn't perish in the heat of the desert, and they camped every night. At times they had to build a road with sticks to get them across the rough terrain. The round trip took a month and a half.

O ne of the best-known sons of New Denmark, New Brunswick, was Winston Bronnum, who learned wood carving as a boy. He graduated to gargantuan concrete sculptures of wildlife, which can be viewed at Animaland, not far from the back entrance to Fundy National Park.

HEAVENS ABOVE!

Dependence in the Maritimes on the land and the sea for a livelihood fostered an awareness of the heavens, both as navigational aids and as forecasters of weather. And, of course, those who spend a lot of time on the open water develop a love of stargazing. Landlubbers who live beyond the city lights tend to have the same love of the skies.

One of my favourite things to do: spread a blanket out on the grass to savour the glories of the northern lights, which bless the rural Maritimes with splendid displays from time to time. It was here that I saw them "crown" for the first time. Something I will never forget. The northern lights are exciting times for ham radio operators, because something in the atmosphere causes radio waves to bounce in from much farther away than normally received.

Thanks to the efforts of a Lower Sackville astronomer, Mary Lou Whitehorne, starry-eyed elementary children in rural schools in Nova Scotia enjoy the wonders of space inside Starlab, a portable, inflatable planetarium. The lab is the baby of the volunteer-run Atlantic Space Sciences Foundation, a charitable organization dedicated to the advance of education in astronomy and space science. The igloo-shaped structure is the size of a classroom and can accommodate 30 children – or fewer adults. Using the lab to learn about the night sky and other things is – to quote the kids – "way cool."

OUR WONDERFUL PARKS

Back down to earth, parks provide pockets of paradise for those who love nature, revere fresh air, have a passion for wilderness and scenic vistas beautiful beyond description. Town, city, provincial or national – each has something unique to offer.

One of Canada's first parks, the Halifax Commons, was granted to the people of Halifax in 1763. Nearby, Canada's oldest public garden, the Halifax Public Gardens, was opened in 1836 by the Nova Scotia Horticultural Society to provide a retreat accessible to all classes.

The Fort Anne National Historic Site in Annapolis Royal is a well-preserved earthenwork fortification dating from 1708 with gunpowder magazines and a museum. The nearby Annapolis Royal Historic Gardens is one of the top display gardens in North America. Highlights include a rose collection, Acadian section, Victorian garden, governors garden, knot garden, perennial border and innovative garden.

Kouchibouguac National Park, on New Brunswick's Acadian shore, boasts spectacular saltwater marshes, lagoons, dunes and golden sandy beaches. It can be explored on hiking trails or bicycle paths or by canoe, kayak or rowboat.

Fundy National Park is a great place to explore the seashore. And you can watch tremendous tides climb up the cliffs and then recede far out on the tidal flats.

Lord Selkirk Provincial Park on Orwell Bay, Prince Edward Island, acknowledges Thomas Douglas, fifth Earl of Selkirk, and his contributions to the area. When Selkirk toured the Highlands of Scotland in 1792, he decided that emigration was the solution to the economic and social problems there. He had bought property on the island, and in July three ships arrived, the Dykes, Polly and Oughton, bringing 800 settlers, from the Isle of Skye, Ross, Argyle, Inverness and Uist. The area was known as Selkirk Settlement for a time.

Doesn't really matter what we call it, truth is that some of the best moments in a Maritimer's life are informal gatherings of neighbours and friends. How it evolves depends on the people: some just hang together and catch a video, whereas others follow tradition and pull out a fiddle to render some foot-stomping, down-home jigs and reels.

We also love to meet and greet our friends and neighbours, and often we attend organized events with just that intention. Hockey games, flea markets, the mall, the theatre – we love them all. And they offer the chance to catch up, to hear the news, the goings on. One of my great joys is living in a provincial capital where I can, on any given day, meet someone I know on the street.

Granted, things have changed in this era of cable TV and satellite dishes. House parties and small gatherings are not as frequent, in spite of easier transportation. On the other hand, the music, song and storytelling – the cultural heart of our people – are reaching a far wider audience. The growing appreciation of the talent in the Maritimes is enabling more and more of our performers to be heard farther afield. We are taking the party to folks everywhere.

CHAPTER 6

ARTS & CULTURE

"To see those splendid young girls manipulating that cloth, – pulling, twisting, turning, rubbing, wringing, lifting, pounding – all to the accompaniment of lilting Gaelic songs. When one set of maidens got tired, it was replaced by another, eager for the job. This whirlwind operation continued for, at least, two hours without intermission; and, when it was all over, that cloth was nearly an inch thick, and guaranteed to wear indefinitely. After, the Fulling Supper was served, and then followed music, dancing, Gaelic songs, and thrilling legendary stories from over the seas. One vied with the other as to which could produce the greatest good cheer."

– J. S. MacDougall,
History of Inverness County

Arts and crafts have always been woven tightly into the fabric of life in the Maritimes. Early Maritimers produced their own tools and equipment, including, for the oxen used on farms and in the woods, yokes, whips and harnesses. Artisans knit fishing nets, wove cloth, built wagons, sewed sails and carved wooden spoons or "skeen" brooms (brooms whittled from a single piece of wood). Many of today's artisans practise skills handed down from those pioneers. Among them are individuals who, through museums and heritage societies, pass on art forms that would otherwise be lost: scrimshaw (carving whale teeth), rope mat weaving, nautical knots, weaving, paper making, woodcarving, model ship building, rug hooking and needlework.

Others turned to recording what they saw and experienced through artistic interpretation and the written word. Music, folk art, books and films have all been part of our cultural development.

It is through performance and celebration that our heritage is kept alive, be it Scottish, Irish, German, French or English. Think of the linking of Cape Breton, with its rich Scottish heritage, to the mainland.

On the day the Canso Causeway officially opened in August 1955, 100 pipers in full tartan marched across the new causeway, skirling "The Road to the Isles," a tune transplanted from Scotland. Scot or not, the sights and sounds must have stirred the soul!

The region has many fine art galleries and gift shops sprinkled along tourist routes. Roadside gift shops as small as a back porch off someone's kitchen or so large they absorb the browser for hours are a good place to seek all manner of handmade goods, folk art and crafts.

But mostly, as my great friend and mentor Silver Donald Cameron has written, "If you want to experience our culture, look in the alternative places." Sure we have all the chain stores and such like the rest of Canada, but the real treasures of the Maritimes are the hidden treasures.

A Stitch at a Time

Needle arts, as they are now known, began with aboriginal porcupine quill work and the elaborate costumes made by the Micmac. Micmac and Maliseet women frequently sold their crafts on the streets of Saint John and Fredericton in the 1800s. Renowned for their quality, their baskets, brooms and moccasins were often awarded prizes at agricultural exhibitions held in the province after 1842.

Early European "plain sewing" included making household linens, making and mending clothes, knitting and other functional work. Even today the warmest socks and mitts that a fisherman has are usually hand-knit. Embroidery, mainly done by well-bred women in the late 18th century and early 19th century, dressed up a gown or a wall hanging. The advent of magazines brought ideas about embroidery, knitting, crochet and even dressmaking to the average household. Ladies' books and magazines gave instructions on how to do needlework. Crochet, known as "poor man's lace," brought both fashion and gentility to many households. For young women, needlework, especially fancy needlework, was considered an ideal evening activity.

Quilting was brought by early European settlers, who practised the craft for utilitarian reasons. Fabric was far too time-consuming to make for extra pieces simply to be thrown away. Worn clothing was remade, and scraps were made into quilts. Crazy quilts were the most common, a simple sewing together of odd scraps with no particular pattern. There are few, if any, original quilt patterns from the Maritimes, other than the "art" pieces now being created. Patterns usually came from England or the United States.

One remarkable crazy quilt, displayed in Cape Breton during a show celebrating the "Year of Needle Crafts," was sewn by Mrs. Caleb Huntington over 100 years ago. Bedridden due to a stoke that left her legs paralyzed, she worked on her quilt for over 10 years. Delicate stitches not only edge each piece but also appear in images embroidered on the fabric. There are chickens, cats, ferns and flowers, as well as the date when the quilt was begun (1887) and the date when it was completed (1897).

Hooked rugs and mats are considered such treasures that a registry has been set up to record both the details of the piece and the history of the maker by the Rug Hooking Guild of Nova Scotia. Old woollen underwear was often incorporated into hooked mats, but the Nova Scotia Museum discovered that it didn't have any in its collection. So a call went out for old sets of Stanfield's, because most Maritimers wore the home-grown undies.

A "Fulling Supper" was a tradition that evolved from the times when women got together in groups to beat raw yarn. As the wool's fibres broke down from their beating, the yarn plumped up -- became "fuller," if you will. After the "fulling," the women would always have supper, as was the custom at these community work sessions. The suppers took on the name of the work being done. Thus a Fulling Supper.

A tapestry incorporating the stories of the Aboriginal people, the British, the French, the Acadians and others who have contributed to the 400-year history of the Annapolis region was recently completed. The Fort Anne Heritage Tapestry, 5.5 metres by 2.3 metres (18 by 7.5 feet), is said to be historically accurate in every detail. It hangs in Annapolis Royal.

"Over one and under two, pull it tight and that will do." The tradition of weaving or braiding wheat and other straw came to Halifax in the 1740s. Straw hats were fashionable in England and Europe, so it wasn't long until settlers were making them both for their own use and to sell. Rush hats, using long, pliable green rushes, were quick to make and were common in areas such as Lunenburg. The art of wheat weaving has undergone a bit of a revival in recent years and can always be found at better craft fairs around Christmas.

Another form of weaving, that used to make eelpots using the withe-rod bush, probably came with English or German settlers in the 1750s. These fishtraps were common in England and Germany. The baskets were also used to gather garden produce, collect cod livers on the fishing schooners and as eel traps in streams and bays. Some withe-rod, or willow, weaving is still done in Lunenburg County, though today the baskets are usually sold as collectors' items. Of course, the most talented basket weavers are the Micmac.

Retirees Doris and David Powell hand-make marionettes, which they sell from their PEI home in a wee shop they call Geppetto's. Anyone can drop in during shop hours and try his or her hand at manipulating the strings. The Powells also make other traditional toys, such as tops.

Canada's first manufacturer of fine crystal products is located on the Halifax waterfront. Nova Scotian Crystal makes crystal in the time-honoured way of mouth blowing and hand cutting – to the delight of visitors who stand with their noses pressed against the glass wall of the studio.

Cavendish Figurines, Canada's first figurine maker, and the only manufacturer of fine earthenware Anne of Green Gables figurines, burst onto the market with its Anne collectibles and has been going strong ever since. The company began with two employees, expanded to nine and in 1998 opened a million-dollar facility at Gateway Village, where Confederation Bridge makes land in Prince Edward Island.

Royal Doulton's pattern Blossom Time celebrates Nova Scotia's beautiful Annapolis Valley.

Each Maritime province has an official tartan or plaid, most of them woven in the region. Jean Reed created the design representative of the PEI landscape, using rust, green, yellow, brown and white to reflect, in the words of Helen Laughlin of Fredericton,

> The warmth and glow of the fertile soil,
> The green of field and tree,
> The yellow and brown of the autumn,
> The white of surf on a summer sea.

Great Northern Knitters, a company that began in a kitchen, now produces 10,000 hand-knit sweaters annually. The Charlottetown company won an Outstanding Exporter Award because of its ability to make products that meet the changing needs of the export market – in this case, traditional fisher's knit sweaters.

Pufferbellies are on the move. Kathi Pettersen of Bridgewater whittled a bar of Ivory soap into a Santa for a grade 6 art contest. Then she wood-carved guppies in grade 8. The tinkering of a child has turned into a solid business, sending Pufferbellies, hand-carved ornaments and custom-made furniture far and wide.

Annie Paul, a Micmac from Indian Brook, Nova Scotia, is the master craftswoman of wooden flowers. She was taught in the 1960s by Madeline Knockwood, who was best known for her wooden rose. Madeline passed away in 1972 at age 79, taking her secret of the construction with her. By learning the process for making other flowers, Annie mastered the art of the wooden rose using feather-thin poplar splints that are hand-cut, dyed and constructed.

Beth Smith, a woodcarver from Indian River in Prince Edward Island, carves full-bloom roses, along with birds, small animals and her first love, horses.

WORDS, WORDS, WORDS!

Perhaps it was the superb early educational systems we had. Perhaps it was the desire to alleviate boredom during the long winters. Perhaps it was a simple love of the written word. Whatever the reason, many early Maritimers were prolific readers and writers. Indeed, the Micmac had a written language before the Europeans arrived. Thankfully, the desire to put word to paper has not diminished, giving our region a proliferation of written material.

Nicholas Denys, an inventive chap, was driven away from the Port Royal area by an "unfriendly" lieutenant-governor. Taking up residence near the Bay of Chaleur, he set up a trading post before moving on to Cape Breton to become governor. He was a skilled observer and writer who produced one of the most detailed accounts of 17th-century Maritimes in a work entitled *The Description and Natural History of the Coasts of North America.*

Simeon Perkins left a valuable legacy. Thanks to his dedication to diary writing, the turbulent days that followed the British captures of Louisbourg and Quebec are documented. His diaries give a remarkable historical record of early life in Nova Scotia. They have been re-published by the Champlain Society, and his home in Liverpool is a museum called Perkins House, adjacent to Queens County Museum. Perkins wrote of the American Revolution, the arrival of the Loyalists and privateering – Liverpool was a real hotbed of that activity!

On March 23, 1752, the type was set for Canada's oldest newspaper, the *Halifax Gazette,* issued by John Bushell, the first king's printer in Halifax. Similar to all early papers, the *Gazette's* existence relied on the government, and most of the content was comprised of government advertisements and official documents. Nine years later, Bushell died, and his partner, Anthony Henry, became editor and king's printer. He got fired for criticizing the Stamp Act, the law by which Britain taxed its colonies to help pay for keeping troops garrisoned. The *Halifax Gazette* was replaced by the semiofficial, subsidized *Nova Scotia Gazette.* Henry then began a rival paper, the *Nova Scotia Chronicle and Weekly Advertiser,* the first newspaper printed independent of government patronage. Within a year, the *Chronicle* took over the *Gazette,* in 1770 becoming the *Nova Scotia Gazette and Weekly Chronicle,* once again with government patronage. Henry was once more editor and king's printer.

Libraries are as much a part of our heritage as sailing ships. It all started in 1606 at Port Royal, when the first settlers read and discussed the books that Marc Lescarbot was proud to lend. A law library was established in Halifax in 1797. The Saint John Public Library is Canada's oldest continuously operating public library in Canada. In 1822 the Yarmouth Book Society was established, beginning the first continuing public library in Nova Scotia.

The name Carnegie tends to be most often linked with music, but for both Canadians and Americans it has a special link to the written word. American industrialist Andrew Carnegie made it possible for thousands of people to access books by funding many libraries, including the Saint John Public Library in 1904. Some folks say that the well-known comic character Jiggs was inspired by Carnegie. Jiggs, the main character in the *Bringing Up Father* strip, was a self-made millionaire married to Maggie, a social-climbing shrew.

Canada's first novel written by a native-born author, Julia Catherine Beckwith Hart of Fredericton, was published in British North America appeared in 1824. She began writing *St. Ursula's Convent; or, The Nun of Canada* when she was 17. It is thought to be a good reflection of life in the era. Only 165 copies were printed.

Judge Thomas Chandler Haliburton, one of North America's first recognized writers of humour, and one of the most quoted authors in the English language, called Windsor, Nova Scotia, home. Apart from his legal career, he wrote substantial works on provincial history, political pamphlets and fiction from 1823 to 1860. But it was *The Clockmaker; or, The Sayings and Doings of Samuel Slick*, of Slickville that made him famous, the first Canadian writer to gain fame outside Canada. "The Clockmaker" appeared in 22 installments in the Novascotian before it was published as a book in 1836. A second and third series followed. It is estimated that as many as 80 editions of *The Clockmaker* appeared during the 19th century. Although Haliburton meant the wisecracks and adventures of Sam Slick to be humorous, he also aimed at showing Nova Scotians how the outside world saw them. His work has been described as "a series of moral essays pointed by satire." *The Old Judge; or, Life in a Colony*, published in 1849, is said to be his finest and most enduring work.

"Thunderin' long words ain't wisdom"
– Thomas Chandler Haliburton, circa 1853.

Beautiful Joe, the (auto)biography of an abused dog, gained author Margaret Saunders international status as a children's writer – the first Canadian to achieve such recognition. Written in 1894, *Beautiful Joe* was the first Canadian book to sell over a million copies. It was published by the American Humane Society and translated into more than 20 languages. Saunders was a prolific writer who dedicated much of her life to the humane treatment of animals, both by treating injured birds at her Halifax home and through illustrated lectures that she travelled far and wide to deliver.

David Walker, author of wonderful stories such as "Wee Geordie," which was later made into a movie, lived in St. Andrews-by-the-Sea after World War II. His wife, Willa Walker, also put pen to paper to capture St. Andrew's glory days in *No Hay Fever and a Railway.*

In 1975, disgusted at being perpetually mistaken for one of the many Donald Camerons who "infest this country," a Cape Breton author adopted the professional name Silver Donald Cameron, a reflection of his prematurely white hair. As the author of 15 books, more than 50 radio dramas, 20 or so TV scripts and innumerable magazine articles, Silver Donald is a highly regarded Maritime writer who has received many awards. A leader in the battle to protect the rights of writers, he is also a columnist with the Halifax *Chronicle-Herald* and the *Globe and Mail.* Dr. Cameron was the first dean of the School of Community Studies at the University College of Cape Breton in Sydney, where he is currently a part-time special assistant to the president.

Carol Burnett, the American queen of laughter, modelled her well-known scrubwoman after an Acadian fictional character created by one of our best-loved authors, Antonine Maillet. Maillet was the winner in 1979 of the prestigious Prix Goncourt for her novel *Pelagie-la-Charrette,* a tale set after the expulsion of the Acadians that symbolizes determination as its heroine struggles to return to Acadia with her cart and cow. The award, the most important literary prize in the French-speaking world, has gained her more international recognition than any other Acadian author.

Singer-songwriter Edith Butler of Paquetville is credited with doing for Acadian music what Maillet did for Acadian literature.

La Sagouine, a remarkable play evoking the lives and spirit of Acadians at the beginning of the century, brought Maillet to the attention of the world in 1960. Her old sage's pithy observations on life in general inspired a theme park, *Le Pays de la Sagouine,* developed on a small island near Buctouche, *Île-aux-Puces* (Isle of Fleas).

The setting is beautiful, colourful and charming. La Sagouine has been portrayed by Viola Léger on stage, in English rather than in her native French if enough of the audience request it.

Henry Alline's *Hymns and Spiritual Songs* are probably the first poems printed in Canada, published by Anthony Henry in 1780. The first edition was published in Halifax, and a fuller version was later published in Boston.

Oliver Goldsmith, nephew of the English writer by the same name, was the first native-born English Canadian to publish a volume of poems, *The Rising Village*. Born in St. Andrews, he wrote the book-length poem describing the rise of a rural village in Nova Scotia as a response to *The Deserted Village,* his English uncle's portrayal of the decline of rural life in Europe. Goldsmith's work was first published in Britain in 1825 and later in Canada.

New Brunswick has fostered a number of important poets, including Sir Charles G. D. Roberts (1860-1943), Bliss Carman (1861-1929) and Alden Nowlan (1933-83). Roberts and Carman were noted for their trips into the province's wilderness in birchbark canoes guided by the Maliseets. Roberts, said to be the first great Canadian poet, was born in Fredericton. He published *Orion and Other Poems* in 1880 and gained immediate popular acclaim. He proved that English Canadian poets could write as well as British ones and became the first Canadian poet to be knighted. He was considered to be a leading scholar and is credited with establishing Canada's first literary movement.

So strong was the poetry community in New Brunswick that a memorial can be found at the University of New Brunswick in Fredericton, dedicated to The Poet's Corner of Canada and the memory of the Confederation Poets.

I really liked what Lowell Thomas and Rex Barton wrote about Carman in their 1939 book *In New Brunswick We'll Find It:*

> "On stormy days when rain whipped against the great French doors and the elms tossed their branches in the gale, Carman mused at his window, absorbing Nature in her violence; distilling it, with pagan understanding, into verses that lesser folk could love."

Shunpiking, from "shunning the turnpikes," is the art of avoiding superhighways and taking sideroads. Apparently, it's a popular way to travel — Shunpiking, the unique name of a Nova Scotia discovery magazine, claims to have 25,000 regular readers.

ANNE OF GREEN GABLES

Prince Edward Island's most famous author, Lucy Maud Montgomery (1874-1942), published 20 novels — remarkably, all still in print — as well as some 500 short stories and poems. Nineteen of her novels are set in Prince Edward Island. She sold her first poem at age 15 and continued to work assiduously at her craft for most of her life. By the late 1890s, she was regularly selling poems and short stories to publications in Canada and the United States. Her first novel, *Anne of Green Gables,* was published in 1908 and became an immediate international success. There are also many books published about her or her work, as far away as Japan and California. Montgomery kept a journal that is now published in a number of books, and it is as compelling as her works of fiction. She had a gift for description and a passion for recording daily life. It is a little-known fact that she was also an avid photographer, buying a camera in the 1890s when her friends were buying bicycles.

Anne of Green Gables, a simple story chronicling the adventures of an orphaned girl who finds an adoptive family on Prince Edward Island, continues to work its magic and bring prosperity to Montgomery's home community, ensuring the preservation of many of the places Montgomery knew so well and loved. Our literary legend lives on in spirit in Park Corner, where her descendants operate the Anne of Green Gables Museum at Silver Bush.

In her journals, Montgomery described the home of her aunt and uncle as "the wonder castle of my childhood." Many of her stories were inspired by the house and farm. The pond on the Campbell farm became the Lake of Shining Waters mentioned in *Anne of Green Gables.* Since the original house was built in 1872, there have been some changes and additions over the years, but recent renovations have restored the house as Montgomery would have known it and have ensured the integrity of the building for years to come. Green Gables House is now a national historic site carefully maintained and administered by Parks Canada.

Perhaps the most spectacular tribute to Montgomery's work is the *Anne of Green Gables* musical, which in 1998 is in the 34th year of a phenomenal run on centre stage at Confederation Centre of the Arts in Charlottetown. The show has played on the world stage as far away as Japan, and has had several cross-Canada tours.

After moving to Leaksdale, Ontario, Montgomery wrote a sequel to *The Story Girl* called *The Golden Road*. One of her favourites, *The Story Girl* was the last book she wrote in Prince Edward Island, seeing her through a time of turmoil and change. Her grandmother was ailing, and her beloved Cavendish home would pass to an uncle. Montgomery was engaged to Reverend Ewan Macdonald, and they would marry, but she was not eager to leave her home province.

These two books formed the framework for the television series *Road to Avonlea*. (Avonlea is the fictional Maritime community made famous in *Anne of Green Gables*.) The series follows the adventures of Sara Stanley, another enchanting heroine.

A second series of novels written by Montgomery, has been turned into another hit television series, *Emily of New Moon*. Montgomery's diaries reveal that her Emily character was the closest to her true story. The captivating tale of a free-spirited girl orphaned at the age of 11 is filmed entirely on location against the breathtaking beauty of the sweeping coastline and rolling fields of Prince Edward Island, giving the series a flawless authenticity. A PEI girl, Martha MacIsaac, plays the lead and another, Jessica Pellerin, her best friend.

There have been several movies of *Anne of Green Gables* made over the years, but two miniseries, now available on video, are the most popular these days.

Reproducing the Anne image has become more complex. The Anne of Green Gables Licensing Authority Incorporated, referred to locally as the Anne Police, has been set up to protect the trademark. For a fee, approved products can be manufactured and sold, with a royalty collected on products manufactured off the island.

Anne and her creator are adored worldwide, but the Japanese take top marks for their dedication. Thousands of Japanese visit Prince Edward Island each year, and the popularity has spawned whole new industries. English-language training schools have popped up in both Japan and Prince Edward Island, where they combine vacation and education. Helen's Homestay, at one end of the spectrum, has students stay in island homes and enjoy "adventure" activities such as cross-country skiing, kayaking, horseback riding – all depending on the season – as well as visit all the Anne sites. Language training focuses each day on activities to take place that day. In Japan correspondence courses from Anne's World offer graduates a trip to the island upon graduation. The Lucy Maud Montgomery Institute offers programs on the University of Prince Edward Island campus during the summer. Houses modelled after Green Gables are marketed in Japan by an island-based company, a Japanese comic strip is based on Anne and in the Maritimes a New Brunswick software developer has come out with an Anne game to play on a computer.

Acadia University offered a course on Canadian literature as early as 1915, one of the first universities in Canada to do so.

Montgomery married in the front parlor of Silver Bush, a home that has become a shrine for many Japanese. The owners received so many requests from Japanese fans who wanted to exchange their own marriage vows in the same room that they now offer complete wedding packages. "My wife still plays the same song – 'The Voice That Breathes o'er Eden,' an old Presbyterian hymn for the Japanese bride as she comes down the stairs," explains George Campbell, a relative of Montgomery. Above the fireplace, the mantel clock – the same one that had to strike 12 times before Montgomery's marriage ceremony could begin – ticks away. The tradition of keeping to the 12th hour is honoured by many Japanese couples who travel to the other side of the world to marry at Silver Bush.

Little could Montgomery have imagined the far-reaching adoration of her work as she sat in her Cavendish bedroom, letting her imagination flow into words on the page.

THE HALIFAX EXPLOSION

December 6, 1917, dawned clear and mild in Halifax. At 7:30 the *Mont Blanc,* a French freighter loaded with benzene, picric acid and TNT, started to move through the Narrows to Bedford Basin, the city's inner harbour. The freighter had come from New York to join the next convoy across the Atlantic. At about 8:00, the *Imo,* a Norwegian tramp steamer carrying relief supplies for Belgium, headed out through the Narrows. In the city, factory workers were already at their jobs. Children were assembling in school playgrounds. Offices and stores were getting ready for the day's business.

As the *Mont Blanc* and the *Imo* drew close to each other, they signalled their intentions. But suddenly the *Mont Blanc* was across the *Imo*'s bow, and at 8:43 the *Imo* rammed the freighter. The two ships drifted apart. People in the city, out enjoying the winter sunshine, watched as a wisp of smoke rose from the harbour. At 9:06 the *Mont Blanc*'s cargo of high explosives ignited.

The explosion was heard as far away as Prince Edward Island. Schools, factories, stores and houses within five kilometres of the ships were completely destroyed. Part of the two-tonne anchor of the *Mont Blanc* was found four kilometres away. Over 1,700 people died, and another 4,000 were injured. That night, with 10,000 people homeless, the temperature plunged to -8°C, and a blizzard was on the way.

One of those shivering with the cold was a 10-year-old boy named John Hugh MacLennan, who would later use that experience as the seed of his first novel, *Barometer Rising,* published in 1941. The native of Glace Bay (who later dropped the John and became just plain Hugh) went on to become one of Canada's most revered and most honoured writers, garnering a drawerful of prizes and honorary degrees, including three Governor General's awards, for his novels *Two Solitudes, The Precipice* and *The Watch That Ends the Night.*

ART FOR ART'S SAKE

Is it the natural beauty that surrounds them? Is it the rich heritage of arts and crafts of all sorts that the Maritimes boast? Whatever, the region has long been home to many of Canada's leading visual artists.

The first photographic studio in British North America was opened in Halifax in 1842 by William Valentine, a portrait painter who became enamoured of the daguerreotype while travelling in Boston. Photography was still in its infancy; only three years had passed since its invention in Paris. During that period, Valentine likely took the first photographs in Canada. The first portrait studio in New Brunswick was opened in Saint John by John Clow, who worked with Valentine.

Another New Brunswicker, George T. Taylor of Fredericton, is considered the pioneer of nature photography, travelling with Maliseet guides into the far reaches of New Brunswick. The heavy photographic equipment of the mid-1800s was carried and dragged into the wilderness using canoes and sleds. What makes his work even more amazing is that he built much of his equipment, including cameras, and developed new processes, such as photographing blueprints. Taylor was also a fine painter and spent the last years of his life working in that medium. Much of his work has been preserved at the New Brunswick Archives in Fredericton.

Peter Barss traces his Nova Scotian ancestry back to Captain Joseph Barss of Lunenburg County, master of a notorious privateer called the Liverpool Packet. Peter, a noted photographer, has captured the work of traditional artisans of Nova Scotia. Many of their skills have been lost, and without the valuable records in his books much of the appreciation for this part of our heritage would also be lost.

The work of legendary Cape Breton photographer Wallace R. MacAskill is as close as the change in your pocket. His 1890 photograph of the *Bluenose* was used as a model for the Canadian dime. Some 100 prints are on display at the MacAskill Museum in St. Peters, and more than 6,000 negatives are on file at the Nova Scotia Archives, providing wonderful documentation of sailing vessels, seascapes, rural life and portraits.

Zwicker's Gallery in Halifax is the oldest commercial art gallery in Canada. The first clients were British military officers in the late 1880s. Descendants of the founder, LeRoy Zwicker, and his wife, Marguerite, are credited with supporting and promoting both Maritime and Canadian artists. Their contribution has been recognized by the establishment of a gallery in their names at the Art Gallery of Nova Scotia. LeRoy was also one of the founders of Arts Canada magazine.

A beautiful little gargoyle, about 40 centimetres high, gives mute testimony to one of Prince Edward Island's best-known early-20th-century artists and art teachers, Mary Allison Doull. Born in 1866 in Wilmot Valley, she studied art before moving to New York in 1894, where she studied further and kept a studio – "One of the cosiest corners… in Fifth Avenue" according to Prince Edward Island Magazine. "Portraits of celebrated men and women, sketches of natural scenery throughout Prince Edward Island and a most hearty welcome greet one upon opening the door."

In 1907 Doull moved to Paris, where she continued her training and exhibited her works. In 1911 she moved back to New York, and for the next 18 years she divided her time between the United States and Prince Edward Island. In 1928 she moved home for good, opening a studio and gallery in an old Methodist church in Cape Traverse. She was especially known for her miniatures and ceramic art. After 1930, when arthritis in her right thumb made it too difficult to paint, she concentrated on pottery and remained an active figure in the arts scene until her death in 1953.

Prince Edward Island's Robert Harris is best known for his painting "The Fathers of Confederation," which burned in the fire that destroyed the Parliament buildings in Ottawa in 1916. Sketches are now being used as the basis for a copy of the painting in oil. Harris portrayed over 200 of the leading personalities of the day. One of his paintings, "A Meeting of the School Trustees," appears in a

Canadian-history vignette shown regularly on television. In 1928 Harris's wife built the Robert Harris Memorial Gallery and Library in Charlottetown. This building was replaced by the Confederation Centre of the Arts, and its gallery houses an extensive collection of Harris works and archives.

William Chritchlow Harris, Robert's brother, directed his creative talents into architecture. His work, particularly the beautiful churches he designed, dots the landscape of the Maritimes. His most famous churches include St. James Anglican Church in Mahone Bay, Nova Scotia, and All Souls' Chapel and his masterwork, St. Paul's Anglican Church, in Charlottetown. He was also responsible for the many white frame churches that are so much a part of the PEI landscape.

Remember *The King and I,* that Broadway musical with Yul Brynner? The real-life "Anna," the teacher who worked with the royal children of Siam, Anna Leonowens, later lived in Halifax. She helped found the Nova Scotia College of Art and Design. An art gallery there bears her name.

The works of two more contemporary artists, Tom Forrestall and Alex Colville, constitute some of the finest modern Canadian painting. Tom, from Middleton, Nova Scotia, and Alex, who was originally from Away but moved for good to the Maritimes when he was nine, studied together at Mount Allison University in Sackville, New Brunswick, in the fifties. Both went on to distinguished careers, fame and fortune, creating memorable images which, for the most part, were based on what they saw around them.

The painter of the picture on our cover, Maud Lewis, came into the world with an unfair proportion of strikes against her. She left it holding a special place in the hearts of those who came in contact with her, and with her work. Her images of cats, oxen, swans, flowers and the places that surrounded her capture, in glorious simplicity, the essence of an era of rural Maritime life.

When she sat in her tiny Digby, Nova Scotia house, in front of an empty canvas, she surely had no knowledge that the colours and images which flowed from her paint brush would gain such far reaching acceptance.

"Maud Lewis is a Nova Scotian icon and a national treasure," wrote Bernard Riordon, Director of the Art Gallery of Nova Scotia. "She embodies the free spirit of folk artists working outside the mainstream, liberated from preconceived notions about art. By creating work that brings joy and reflects simplicity, Maud Lewis succeeded in illuminating the best of the human spirit."

My own thoughts about Maud would be expressed in perhaps less lofty language, but equal admiration and respect. She was a lady who had a lot of life's curve balls thrown at her. She met them head on, and in her own quiet unassuming way not only satisfied her own creative drive, but also made the world a brighter, happier place.

My introduction to Maud and her work came when I was a fledgling lifestyles editor at our local newspaper. Lance Woolaver, came in looking for a story on his two little books, *From Ben Loman to the Sea* and *Christmas With the Rural Mail,* both illustrated with Maud Lewis images. He had many childhood recollections of Maud. His teacher acted as Maud's "secretary" mailing her paintings to buyers far afield. His father was Maud's patron, buying a promoting her paintings. His passion for the artist lit mine.

"When we went to pick them up, I was amazed to see that the interior of the house was decorated with the same swans, robins, and flowers as the exterior. There were cornflowers on the steps to the attic, daisies on the cast iron stove, and a little burro and siesta scene on the side of a desk. Maud's paintings were drying, propped up around her, where the light of the window could catch them. On a rainy day the new ones sat on the warming oven of the stove."

Born in 1903 in South Ohio, Maud suffered from multiple birth defects that left her shoulders unnaturally sloped and her chin resting on her chest. An older Maud was described as having arms and hands that were "twisted and crippled" and a bent frame, perhaps because of a stint with polio.

Her father was a blacksmith, farmer and harness maker – a respected craftsman. Her mother nurtured and protected Maud giving her her first instruction in art. They painted Christmas cards which they sold door-to-door. Such endeavours were a common practice in those days. Hers was a happy childhood, and Maud bright-eyed, eager and talented. The happy home, pets, music and surroundings are reflected in her work.

Maud married Everett Lewis at age 34. Stories differ about who courted whom. What is known is that she took a step down the economic ladder, moving from comfort to a "cracker-box" with one-room and an attic sleeping loft. This little cottage became her studio, her home and even her canvas for the next 32 years.

Although when they married it was the intention that Maud take on the household duties, rheumatoid arthritis twisted her hands into the shape of lobster claws thwarting Everett's plans for a capable housekeeper. He assumed those duties but never made any improvements to the home, not even electricity, even though he was a master scrounger and had money in the bank. They lived simply and almost totally off the land. Maud contribution came through her art. Everett took paintings along when he peddled fish.

When Maud hung out a "Paintings for Sale" sign with red-breasted bluebirds and pink apple blossoms, the effect was astonishing. Drivers slowed down to enjoy the fantastic sight of her biggest canvas, their tiny home had daffodils painted on the windows, blue birds and swans on the doors. Many stopped to buy a painting.

It worked well. While Maud painted, Everett tended house, stove and garden. They greeted those who came to buy Maud's work together, but Everett, who loved to peddle and haggle, handled the money.

She moved from cards to painting on boards with oils – often using salvaged paint found by Everett, particularly during the war when supplies were scarce. The habit of south shore Acadians to paint their homes and boats with such bright colours was a bonus for Maud. She developed a style that was uniquely Maud Lewis. Three legged cows, eyelashes on oxen, colourful trees resplendent in fall red leaves in snowscapes; all manner of inconsistencies and eccentricities, gave her work a hallmark of her own unique style.

She spent most of her life comfortably seated in her chair by the window in a cheerful corner, Maud painted and watched the world come and go. She rarely painted people, but when she did it was almost always a tall thin man dressed for the woods or fields with a red cap with ear flaps and black mittens – obviously Everett. He was a man with faults, but he cared for Maud and made it possible for her to leave a rich legacy which will be treasured for all time. He made it possible for her to do what she loved best: paint.

THE GIFT OF MUSIC

It was the Micmac, of course, who created the first music to be heard in the forest-covered hills and along the coastal waters of the Maritimes. The music of the Acadians, Highland Scots, English, Germans and many other groups have added to that of the Micmac to enrich our musical heritage.

During the Victorian era, band music was extremely popular. The town of Truro formed an amateur band as early as 1852. Out of this interest grew the well-known Truro Citizen's Band, which stirred townspeople with marches and public outdoor concerts. That music may have inspired Truro native Albert Earl McNutt to pen his popular World War I song "We'll Never Let the Old Flag Fall."

A boy was born in Brooklyn, Nova Scotia, in 1914, one of six children. Little Clarence Eugene Snow spent much of his childhood suffering abuse at the hands of a mean grandmother and stepfather. At 12 he was "booted out" and headed to sea on a fishing schooner. The fishermen became his family and the sea his home until he was nearly killed in a shipwreck. Years later he established the Foundation for the Prevention of Child Abuse in his own name: Hank Snow.

Snow began entertaining on the boats, saved for months for his first guitar and developed his unique style. In 1936, now known as Hank the Yodelling Ranger, he became Canada's bestselling artist. He performed coast to coast, but the financial rewards were few – his first royalty cheque from RCA was for $1.96. He headed south across the border and in 1950 joined the Grand Ole Opry. He was about to be dropped when "I'm Movin' On" hit the charts. Snow went on to become one of the biggest stars in country music, recording over 140 albums and 833 commercial sides. His greatest hits: "I'm Movin' On," his signature song, "The Golden Rocket," "Rhumba Boogie," "Bluebird Island," "Down the Trail of Achin' Hearts," "Music-Makin' Mama from Memphis," "The Gold Rush Is Over," "Lady's Man," "I Went to Your Wedding," "Yellow Roses," "I Don't Hurt Anymore," "Beggar to a King," "Hello, Love."

Anyone with a love for country music should plan a visit to the Hank Snow Country Music Centre in Liverpool, Nova Scotia, which showcases Snow and other artists.

In 1928 a young writer named Helen Creighton was asked to research a story about Nova Scotia's pirates. She didn't know any local pirate stories, so she drove to Eastern Passage, where she met Enos Hartlan, who not only told pirate stories but also sang pirate songs. Helen reasoned that, if one person knew so many songs, there must be many more. Thus began the life's work of the woman known as "Canada's First Lady of Folklore."

Creighton worked until her death in 1989, amassing the largest individual folklore collection in Canada: it includes approximately 16,000 songs reflecting the diverse ethnic and cultural backgrounds of Nova Scotians. There are Micmac songs from Shubenacadie Reserve, Acadian songs from West Pubnico and Cheticamp, ancient British ballads, German songs in Lunenburg County, Gaelic songs of Irish and Scottish heritage and songs of slavery such as "No More Auction Block for Me." Sea captains from Yarmouth sang shanties for Creighton, without the aid of what the old salts used to call rusty water (dark rum). They were all members of the local temperance society. There are songs of the supernatural, such as "The Ghostly Sailors," still believed by many to bring bad luck if sung at sea or on shore. And there are songs about the tragic "Springhill Mining Disaster" and "The Halifax Explosion."

Truro native Portia White was a contralto who became the first black Canadian woman to win acclaim on the international concert stage. Raised in a musical family with 13 children, she sang in her father's African Baptist Church on Cornwallis Street in Halifax as a child. Her international debut came in 1944 at the prestigious New York Town Hall. Under contract with Columbia Concerts Incorporated, she could sing in five languages and did so around the world. She gave a command performance for Queen Elizabeth II and performed more than 100 concerts in her career. A plaque at the Black Cultural Centre, formally recognized by the Historic Sites and Monuments Board of Canada, commemorates her accomplishments, which are said to be "of national significance in the history of Canada."

Lord Beaverbrook was a great lover of local songs. During World War II, he would burst into song at gatherings of international politicians seeking to win the war. His favourite tune, "The Jones

Boys," a simple Miramichi song about some boys who lived at Jones Crossing, New Brunswick, has been sung by such unlikely figures as Sir Winston Churchill and Russian Vyacheslav Mikhailovich Molotov. Some people say that Molotov loved to belt it out because he thought it emphasized the downfall of capitalism. But "The Jones Boys" only pokes fun at some local boys:

> I'll tell you a tale of the Jones Boys
> Who lived in yonder hill,
> Two jolly fellows with a twinkle in their eye,
> And they did each own a mill.
> They owned a mill in the side of a hill,
> And Eliza she worked in the kiln.
> They worked all night, and they worked all day,
> But they couldn't make the gosh-darned sawmill pay.
> Then hi dum diddle um Johnny Jones,
> Then hi dum diddle um Jimmy.

Reality is that the Jones boys were quite successful, but locals liked to have some fun with them. Beaverbrook actually installed a set of bells at the University of New Brunswick that are known to peal out the tune.

For almost four decades, the old-time music of *Don Messer and The Islanders* brought traditional fiddle and dance into homes across Canada. New Brunswick born, Don Messer (1909-73) began fiddling at age five, and by seven he was performing. He began his radio career in Saint John in 1929, moving it to Charlottetown in 1939, where he formed The Islanders for CFCY. Some members of The Islanders changed, but others were the constants whom many came to love so well: Marg Osborne, Charlie Chamberlain, Duke Nielsen, Ray Simmons, Warren MacRae and Waldo Munro.

When the CBC cancelled the show in 1969, after a 10-year run, the public outcry was so strong that the show was syndicated from CHCH – TV in Hamilton until Messer's death in 1973. One of his greatest contributions was the exposure provided for young artists such as Stompin' Tom Connors and Catherine McKinnon.

Stompin' Tom Connors, the foot-stomping singer, songwriter and guitarist, was born in New Brunswick and grew up in Skinners Pond, Prince Edward Island. He sang for his living when he found himself broke in Timmins, Ontario, and went on to become a star. The foot pounding that is his trademark began in an effort to be heard above the din of a noisy bar.

It's a long way from the small town of Springhill, Nova Scotia, to the entertainment capitals of the world, but Anne Murray found her way. Her rich alto voice has taken her around the world and into the hearts of millions of fans. It was her rendition of Gene MacLellan's "Snowbird" that launched her international career in 1970. It still brings people to their feet. The first single recorded by a Canadian female performer to go gold in the United States, it was the first of many hits. Anne's warm voice, relaxed delivery and diverse repertoire have earned her fans in musical categories from gospel to rock.

With over 25 Juno Awards, four Grammy Awards and numerous gold and platinum records, Murray stands as one of Canada's most successful recording stars. In honour of her contribution to the advancement of Canada's performing arts, she was awarded the Order of Canada. Her greatest hits include "Snowbird," "Danny's Song," "Put Your Hand in the Hand," "You Needed Me" and "I Just Fall in Love Again."

Murray retains close ties to her hometown, visiting every summer. The Anne Murray Centre chronicles her life and career with a collection of award-winning exhibits called "From Springhill to the World."

There's no denying that a lot has changed for the woman who, as a child, had to drop her singing lessons because she was too shy to let out a note. Rita MacNeil, one of eight children, grew up in tiny Big Pond, Cape Breton. An artist now known worldwide for her wide-ranging styles – Celtic, country, folk, R & B, blues and rock – MacNeil left home at age 17 to pursue her dream of becoming a singing star.

She moved to Ontario, but after more than a decade there, along with marriage, divorce and two children, she wanted to leave. She says that her years of struggling to make ends meet by working low-end jobs and singing where she could have been a great inspiration for her songwriting. Homesick, she tried to make it home every summer. One year, in the late 1970s, she decided to stay, and that was when her career took a better direction. Moving home seemed to open up her writing as she became reacquainted with her roots. Connecting with musicians from home brought everything into focus for her.

MacNeil released her early albums independently. *Born a Woman,* her first album (1975), was put out with the help of friends who collected money to finance the project. She went on to record independently *Flying on Your Own,* attempting unsuccessfully to get the major record labels interested. Not one to give up easily, MacNeil went ahead and released the album herself, selling so many copies that record companies rallied around her. To date, she has received five honorary doctorates and won three Juno Awards and four Canadian Country Music Awards. One of her proudest moments was being inducted into the Order of Canada in 1992.

St. Mary's Church in Indian River, Prince Edward Island, has acoustics that musicians from all over the world deem "near perfect," which explains why high-calibre performers, particularly classical musicians, travel long distances to play before audiences or to record their music.

Those who visit Cape Breton Island never forget it. Bagpiping and fiddling fill the air when local musicians gather to celebrate their heritages on the shores and in the villages. Ceilidh (kay-lee) is Gaelic for "party" or "gathering," and that is exactly what you will find on the Ceilidh Trail. The Celtic Colours International Festival, held in the fall, is just one of many chances to enjoy great music and great fun. Cape Breton is known for its wealth of Celtic music and dance, so it seems strange that at one time there was an edict against dance. It was prohibited by church authorities.

Achievement in Scottish music is not limited to Cape Breton. Consider these young musicians from Summerside's College of Piping. Piper John MacPhee won a North American invitational in Connecticut and a YTV Achievement Award in 1998. He's 17. Michael Linkletter was the North American Solo Piping Champion in 1994, and Patricia Murray won a top award, Gaelic Mod, for singing in Inverness, Scotland, in Gaelic in 1997. The school's pipe band was North American Champion in 1995. The college has released three recordings.

The biggest musical party we have is the East Coast Music Awards, an event that celebrated its 10th anniversary in 1998. A week of music, business and what one seasonal delegate called social mayhem moves from province to province to showcase new talent and reward stars. Typically, every performance area in the host city is transformed into a minifestival.

The Men of the Deep, the first choir of coal miners in North America, based in Glace Bay since 1966, performs in miner's gear, helmets, lights and all. Working or retired miners, they have a number of albums to their credit and are best known for performing with Anne Murray and Rita MacNeil.

Roch Voisine (Joseph Armand), known now as a Quebecois singer-songwriter, was born in Saint-Basile, New Brunswick. European tours and his single "I'll Always Be There" made Voisine an international success, with sales exceeding 1 million. To date he has sold more than 6 million records worldwide.

One of the first Tracker pipe organs in North America can be seen at the neogothic St. Simon and St. Jude Catholic Church (built in 1860) in Tignish, Prince Edward Island. The organ was constructed in 1882 by Louis Mitchell.

"Eccentric," "charismatic," "energetic," "evolutionary." These are all words that have been used to describe hot young fiddling phenom Ashley MacIsaac, who turned the music world on its ear with his debut album, *Close to the Floor,* produced in 1992 when he was only 17. What does Ashley have to say about all this hype? "I basically want to make a lot of money as quick as I can, and then go back to playing square dances in Cape Breton."

Holly Cole, jazz singer extraordinaire, and her brother, Alan Cole, musician and composer, grew up in Fredericton. Other notable musicians with Maritime connections include Carroll Baker,

The Rankin Family, Sarah McLachlan (the 1998 *Chatelaine* Woman of the Year) and Wilf Carter.

The Play's The Thing

Some of the best theatre in the country is to be found in the Maritimes. Larger stages, such as at the Neptune Theatre in Halifax and the Confederation Centre of the Arts in Charlottetown, are joined by dozens of smaller venues, which are amazing for their longevity and the talent they bring to the stage. In the summer in most of the Maritimes, you are within an easy drive to some sort of stage production.

Marc Lescarbot, a French lawyer and writer, spent the winter of 1606-07 at the settlement of Port-Royal in Nova Scotia. A member of Samuel de Champlain's *Ordre de Bon Temps* (Order of Good Cheer), he was involved with the entertainment that each man provided to the group. Although a published poet and historian, it was his masque that gained him a place in Canadian history. The play, with music and dialogue, *Le Théâtre de Neptune en la Nouvelle-France* (The Theatre of Neptune in New France) welcomed Sieur de Poutrincourt and Champlain back to Port-Royal after an exploratory voyage that took them as far as Martha's Vineyard. It was the first non-Native theatrical presentation in North America north of Mexico. That first version was performed by a cast of 11 settlers on several small boats in mid-November, making it the first floating show as well.

In 1962 a regional repertory theatre opened in Halifax and was named the Neptune Theatre in honour of Lescarbot's pioneer performance. Productions of his play are still put on at the theatre.

Citizens of Saint John have always loved theatre and cinema. Mallard House, home of the Legislative Assembly from 1786 to 1797, also housed theatrical performances. There were six motion picture houses in 1913, more than in any other centre in the Maritimes, making Saint John one of the best show towns in Eastern Canada. Live theatre goes back even further. Lillie Langtry, the famed beauty, stage star and mistress of Edward VII, performed in Saint John at the Mechanics' Institute in 1883. The Jersey Lillie, as she was known, played to rave reviews.

Fingall O'Flahertie Wills, a.k.a. Oscar Wilde, who appeared on stage in Saint John in 1882, was apparently enamoured of Lillie; he wrote poems referring to her as the new Helen of Troy. Wilde presented lectures on aesthetics in home decor. Adorned in a velvet jacket, knee breeches, silver-buckled shoes — the attire of a dandy in Europe – he was scorned and ridiculed, just as he scorned and ridiculed the homes of the city.

·On The Screen & ·Over The Airwaves

The first dramatic feature-length motion picture made in Canada was about our own Evangeline. Made in Halifax in 1913, it told the tale of Longfellow's Acadian heroine at the time of the expulsion. Many of the scenes were shot on location in the Annapolis Valley to keep the film as accurate as possible. It was a box office success and received critical acclaim, but it wasn't enough to keep the filmmaker, Canadian Bioscope Company, in business past 1915.

Saint John has had its fair share of famous sons who have made their mark on the silver screen. Walter Pidgeon was known locally as a fine young baritone before he made his way to Hollywood. There he apparently gave up crooning a fine tune for more romantic roles. Donald Sutherland has appeared in varied roles in dozens of films. His most notable roles, to me at least, both portrayed healers: Norman Bethune and one of the wacky medical heroes in the original *MASH* movie. And Hollywood tycoon Louis B. Mayer, the son of a junk dealer, was considered the most powerful producer in Hollywood for 25 years. The steps that took a skinny kid to a position as a filmmaking mogul in tinsel town would themselves make a movie. Mayer began operating movie theatres and by 1916 had formed a production company that became known as Metro-

Goldwyn-Mayer (MGM). In the 1930s and 1940s, Mayer was the most powerful magnate in Hollywood. His annual salary of $1.25 million made him the highest-paid person in the United States. He wasn't particularly popular and was ousted in a power struggle in 1951, six years before his death. Among his more famous lines: "Look out for yourself or they'll pee on your grave." Among his best films: *The Big Parade* (1925), *Ben Hur* (1926), *Grand Hotel* (1932) and *Dinner at Eight* (1933). The Jewish Historical Museum in Saint John is a must stop for Mayer fans.

Ruby Keeler, born in Halifax in 1909, danced in a speakeasy and on Broadway before making her film debut in *42nd Street* opposite newcomer Dick Powell. She and Powell were teamed in seven Warner Brothers films. She married music star Al Jolson. Ruby retired from the screen in 1941 and, after occasional TV appearances in the 1950s and 1960s, made one of the most heralded show business comebacks, charming Broadway in the 1971 revival of the musical NoNo Nanette.

If "Just Mary" or a red-haired moppet named Maggie Muggins mean anything to you, then read on! Fredericton schoolteacher Mary Grannan created the characters, along with Mary's friend Fitzgerald the Fieldmouse, and told stories of their exploits on CBC radio and television from 1939 to 1962. She also published them in books.

Filmmaker Don Shebib, originally from the Sydney area, is famous for directing *Goin' Down the Road,* the story of two Maritimers who migrate to Toronto in search of a better life.

Actor Harold Russell, also from Sydney, is the only actor ever to win two Oscars for the same role. He volunteered as an instructor and demolitions expert during World War II. During a demonstration on assembling explosives, a defective blasting cap detonated and cost him both hands. He appeared in an army documentary, *The Diary of a Sergeant,* which depicts the rehabilitation of an amputee, then was chosen to play a key role in *The Best Years of Our Lives,* winning the 1946 Academy Award for Best Supporting Actor for his performance as an amputee struggling to adjust to civilian life as well as a second, special Academy Award "for bringing hope and courage to his fellow veterans." Russell helped to organize the World Veterans Federation. An annual award presented by the President's Committee on Employment of People with Disabilities is called the Harold Russell Medal. In 1993 Russell became the first Academy Award winner to auction an Oscar (for $125,000).

The first American film made about Canada, An Acadian Elopement, came out in 1907.

The streets in the movie *Children of a Lesser God* may appear familiar to those from Saint John, for filming took place in Rothesay and on the nearby coast. Marlee Matlin won an Oscar for Best Actress.

The CBC Television series *Black Harbour* has brought prosperity to the south-shore Nova Scotian community of Mill Cove, which suffered an economic blow when the Canadian Forces Base there closed in the early 1990s. *Black Harbour* generates more money in the community than the military did and is thus indicative of the importance of the film industry to the region.

The following stars have — or have had – summer homes in Nova Scotia: Jack Nicholson, Alan Arkin, Christopher Reeve, Paul Simon, Tom Cruise and Nicole Kidman, Bruce Willis and Demi Moore, Billy Joel, Roger Moore and James Brolin.

A Titanic Event

The most newsworthy film event in recent years in the Maritimes is, without a doubt, *Titanic.* Director James Cameron pulled Halifax and its citizens into the excitement in ways that no one could have anticipated. Based in Halifax, Cameron made 12 dives to the wreck of the *Titanic* and, using what he called a "cheesy Hollywood robot," did the shots for the movie. That the modern-day scenes were filmed in Halifax during the summer of 1996 was exciting, but the excitement was nothing compared to that after the film opened.

The movie has brought people flocking to Halifax seeking the last resting place of the victims of the disaster. The Halifax crews and undertakers who braved ice and waves to recover victims brought home horrific tales, "wreckwood souvenirs" and more than 200 bodies. The grave of "victim 227 J. Dawson," apparently one of *Titanic*'s engine-room workers, aged 23, has attracted many visitors to the Fairview Cemetery, one of three Halifax burial grounds used in 1912. An unexpected legacy of the mass death was the skillfully improvised system of identifying bodies that proved invaluable in 1917, when the city itself suffered almost 2,000 deaths in the Halifax Explosion. Visitors also flock to the Maritime Museum of the Atlantic, where the Nova Scotian perspective on the disaster takes on an eerie reality. Halifax undoubtedly has one of the most moving links to the tragedy, brought to life by the presence of a delicately carved newel post from the famous staircase and an elegant but empty deck chair, the only intact *Titanic* deck chair in the world. The interest in these sites inspired by the movie has been so intense that it has kick-started some major development and restoration – a good thing for Haligonians.

The Titanic was one of the first ships to use the newly adopted distress signal SOS.

Everyone who sees *Titanic* will recall the hero's sketches of the heroine long after leaving the theatre. So where did the beautiful sketches and art seen in the movie come from? From Halifax artist Marilyn McAvoy. She met Cameron on the Halifax shoot, working with him to age his own drawing of Kate Winslet. Later that summer, McAvoy was in a hotel room in Prince Edward Island painting portraits needed for *Emily of New Moon* when a man knocked on her door with a message from Mexico. Cameron needed her. She flew to Mexico to create "non-existent works in the style of famous artists" for the set. She stayed for six months as the on-set or standby painter. McAvoy actually appeared in the movie as the lab technician who reveals the drawing found in a portfolio at the bottom of the ocean. She also did the sketches that Rose discovers when she flips through Jack's sketchbook.

Celtic Revival

The influence of Celtic arts and culture in Maritime life cannot be overstated. Perhaps it's most visible – I guess that should be audible – in the music. A couple of institutions, along with many more informal groups and societies, are dedicated to ensuring that the Celtic cultural thread is never lost.

Summerside's College of Piping has developed a reputation as an international school for the study of Highland bagpiping and other Celtic arts. Students come from as far away as New Zealand, Singapore, Germany, the United States and, yes, even Scotland. The college also sells all manner of clan and highland stuff, such as kilts, drumming supplies and even bagpipes. And during the summer the school puts on Highland gatherings, concerts, military tattoos and, of course, ceilidhs, which are an excellent showcase for students and provide visitors with terrific entertainment.

The Gaelic College of Celtic Arts and Crafts in Cape Breton was founded in 1938 in a log cabin. Today it has international recognition for its contribution to the preservation of Gaelic and of Celtic arts and culture. Subjects include Cape Breton fiddle, Celtic harp, weaving, accordion and all manner of piping and dancing. The college's Great Hall of the Clans is visited by over 8,000 people annually, looking to trace the history and development of the Celts.

Where do you Stop?

Pound for pound, person for person, Maritimers have to be the most creative people on God's green earth. And the most modest!

THE END

If this book has whet your appetite for the Maritimes, then don't hesitate to pay us a visit. There is so much more to see and do!

We've just scratched the surface enough to tickle your interest. I would be fully confident in saying that each and every one of the topics touched on within these pages could be developed into a chapter of its own, or even into a full book.

There are two kinds of people in this life. Those who just pass through and those who take time to stop, to savour, to create memories and to taken them out from time to time to enjoy over and over again. It was my intention when writing this book to give you something that falls into the stop and savour category, to create memories that will make your own experience of, and appreciation for, the Maritimes the best it can be.

But more than anything I hope the tidbits of history, the snippets of information about great people, encourages a deeper appreciation of the region that we call home – the Maritimes – one of Canada's most illuminating jewels.

Sources

In compiling a book of this nature I have obviously benefitted from the work of many other hands who have come before me. Here are some.

BOOKS

1867 Canada 1967 - The Centennial Food Guide: A Century of Good Eating by Pierre and Janet Berton, McClelland and Stewart, Toronto, 1966; *A Century of Canadian Home Cooking* by Carol Ferguson & Margaret Fraser, Prentice Hall Canada, Scarborough, 1992; *A Taste of Acadia* by Marielle Cormier-Boudrea and Melvin Gallant; *An Historical Almanac of Canada* by Lena Newman, Goose Lane Editions, Fredericton, NB, 1991; *An Island Scrapbook* by Benjamin Bremner, self-published, Charlottetown, 1932; *Atlantic Canada At the Dawn of a New Nation* by E. Boyde Beck, Greg Marquis, Joan M. Payzant and Shannon Ryan, Windsor Publications, Burlington, ON, 1990; *Book of Canadian Winners & Heroes* by Brenna and Jeremy Brown, Prentice-Hall Canada, Scarborough, ON, and Newcastle Publishing Limited, Toronto, 1983; *Canadian Yesterdays* by Edgar A. Collard, Longmans Canada, Toronto, 1955; *Canada Firsts* by Ralph Nader, McClelland and Stewart, Toronto, 1992; *Canada's Maritime Provinces* by Benoit Prieur, Ulysses Travel Publications, 1995; *Canada - The Twentieth Century* by Fred McFadden, Don Quinlan and Rick Life, Fitzhenry & Whiteside, Toronto, 1982; *Canada Unlimited* by Gerald Anglin, The O'Keefe Foundation, Toronto, 1948; *Dictionary of Prince Edward Island English* by T. K. Pratt, University of Toronto Press, Toronto, 1988; *Down Memory Lane* by H. M. MacDonald, Charlottetown, PEI; *Evangeline: The Story of the Acadian Expulsion of 1755,* intro. by C. Bruce Fergusson, Nimbus Publishing, Halifax, 1951; *Exploring Nova Scotia* by Lance Feild, Fast & McMillan Publishers, Charlotte, NC, 1927; *Faces and Places: Travel and Tales in Nova Scotia's Antigonish and Guysborough Counties* by Terry Tremayne, Tremayne Associated, Halifax, 1983; *Favourite Recipes From Old Prince Edward Island* by Julie V. Watson, Nimbus Publishing, Halifax, 1986; *Flashback Canada* by J. Bradley Cruxton and W. Douglas Wilson, Oxford University Press, Toronto, 1987; *Folklore of Nova Scotia* by Mary L. Fraser, Formac, Antigonish, n.d.; *Food - à la canadienne,* Canadian Dept of Agriculture, Ottawa, 1976; *From the Hearth* by Hope Dunton, University College of Cape Breton Press, Sydney, 1986; *Gems of Fancy Cookery* by J. D. Copeland, J. D. Copeland, Druggist, Antigonish, n.d.; *Ghosts and Legends of Prince Edward Island* by Julie V. Watson, Hounslow Press, Toronto, 1988; *Gold in Nova Scotia* by Jennifer L. E. Bates, Nova Scotia Dept of Mines and Resources, 1997; *Halifax: Warden of the North* by Thomas H. Raddall, McClelland and Stewart, Toronto, 1971; *Heritage Recipes (Atlantic Insight),* Formac, 1988; *In New Brunswick We'll Find It* by Lowell Thomas and Rex Barton, D. Appleton-Century, New York/London, 1939; *It Happened In Canada* by Gordon Johnston, Methuen, Agincourt, ON, 1983; *Journey Through Nova Scotia...* (York, 1774), reprinted in the Report of the Public Archives of Nova Scotia, 1944-45; *Lebanese Peoples of the Maritimes* by Dr. Joseph G. Jabbra and Dr. W. Jabbra, Four East Publications, Tantalon, NS, 1987; *Legends, Oddities & Mysteries ... including UFO experiences in New Brunswick* by Dorothy Dearborn, Neptune, Saint John, NB, 1996; *Local History in Atlantic Canada* by William B. Hamilton, Macmillan of Canada, Toronto, 1974; *Marie Nightingale's Favourite Recipes* by Marie Nightingale, Nimbus, Halifax, 1993; *Maritime Firsts: Historic Events, Inventions & Achievements* by Dan Soucoup, Pottersfield Press, Lawrencetown Beach, NS, 1996; *McAlpine's Gazetteer,* Union Assurance Society, England, n.d.; *Metepenagiag: New Brunswick's Oldest Village* by Patricia Allen, Red Bank First Nation/Goose Lane Editions, Fredericton, NB, 1994; *Myths & Legends Beyond Our Borders* by Charles M. Skinner; *No Place Like Home: Diaries and Letters of Nova Scotia Women 1771-1938* by Margaret Conrad, Toni Laidlaw and Donna Smyth, Formac, Halifax,1988; *No Place Like Home* by Mary K. MacLeod, University College of Cape Breton, Sydney, NS, 1992; *North Along the Shore* by Edith Mosher, Lancelot Press, Windsor, NS, 1975; *Nova Scotia: A Brief History* by Phyllis R. Blakeley, J. M. Dent & Sons (Canada), Toronto, 1955; *Nova Scotia: A Colour Guidebook* by Stephen Poole, Formac, Halifax, 1994; *Off-Trail in Nova Scotia* by Will R. Bird, McGraw-Hill Ryerson, Toronto, 1956;

Older Ways: Traditional Nova Scotian Craftsmen by Peter Barss and Joleen Gordon, Van Nostrand Reinhold, Toronto, 1980; *Outstanding Women of Prince Edward Island*, Zonta Club, Charlottetown, PEI, 1981; *Pirates & Outlaws of Canada, 1610-1932* by Harold Horwood and Ed Butts, Doubleday Canada, Toronto, 1984; *Prince Edward Island Colour Guide,* edited by Laurier Brinklow, Formac, Halifax, 1995; *Reader's Digest Heritage of Canada,* The Reader's Digest Association (Canada), Montreal, 1978; *Roads to Remember: The Insider's Guide to New Brunswick* by Colleen Whitney Thompson, Goose Lane, Fredericton, 1994; *Shipwrecks & Seafaring Tales of Prince Edward Island* by Julie V. Watson, Hounslow Press, Toronto, 1994; *Tales Told in Canada* by Edith Fowke, Doubleday Canada, Toronto, 1986; *The Atlantic Cookbook* by the contributors and readers of Atlantic Insight, edited by Patricia Holland, Formac, Halifax, 1987; *The Avonlea Album* by Fiona McHugh, Firefly Books, Willowdale, ON, 1991; *The Canadian Encyclopedia*, Hurtig, Edmonton, 1985; *The Elegant Canadians* by Luella Creighton, McClelland and Stewart, Toronto, 1967; *The Fascinating World of New Brunswick* by Stuart Trueman, McClelland and Stewart, Toronto, 1973; *The Illuminated Life of Maud Lewis* by Lance Woolaver and Bob Brooks, Nimbus/Art Gallery of Nova Scotia, Halifax, 1996; *The Maritime Country Diary* by Susan Perry and Joe McKendy, Nelson Canada, Toronto, 1981; *The Maritimes: Tradition, Challenge & Change,* edited by George Peabody, Carolyn MacGregor and Richard Thorne, Maritext, Halifax, 1987; *The Norman MacLeod Heritage Series,* Gaelic College of Celtic Arts and Crafts, St. Ann's, NS, 1996; *The Real Klondike Kate* by T. Ann Brennan, Goose Lane, Fredericton, 1990; *The Story of Prince Edward Island* by P. Blakeley and M. Vernon, J.M. Dent & Sons (Canada), Toronto, 1963; *The Strawberry Connection* by Beatrice Ross Buszek, Nimbus, Halifax, 1984; *The Third Maritime Reader,* W. M. Collins, Sons, Glasgow, London and Edinburgh, n.d.; *The Will to Win: Ron Turcotte's Ride to Glory* by Bill Heller, Fifth House, Saskatoon, 1992; *These Are The Maritimes* by Will R. Bird, The Ryerson Press, Toronto, 1959; *This is Nova Scotia* by Will R. Bird, McGraw-Hill Ryerson, Toronto, 1950; *Two Cooks in the Kitchen* by Janet Bell and Janet Lee, Pottersfield Press, Porters Lake, NS, 1990.

PERIODICALS

Atlantic Gig; Atlantic Progress; Cape Breton's Magazine (several issues); *Shunpiking; The Atlantic Advocate; The Canadian Magazine; The Cape Breton Post* (Sydney, NS); *The Chronicle-Herald* (Halifax); *The Coast; The Guardian* (Charlottetown); *The Halifax Herald; The Journal Pioneer* (Summerside, PEI); *The Mail Star - The Chronicle Herald* (Halifax); *The Pictou Advocate* (Pictou, NS); *The Prince Edward Island Magazine* (1899-1905); *Times Transcript* (Moncton); *What's Goin' On? Cape Breton's Arts & Entertainment Magazine.*

THE OTHERS

Capital Commission of P.E.I.; The Gaelic College of Celtic Arts and Crafts; New Brunswick Tourism; Nova Scotia Dept of Natural Resources; Nova Scotia Museums; Nova Scotia Tourism; Parks Canada; PEI Potato Board; Prince Edward Island Museum and Heritage Foundation; Prince Edward Island Tourism; United Mine Workers of America, District 26; Lorne Johnston (the Ole Salt); Helen Grant; Debbie Gamble-Arsenault; Silver Donald Cameron; Beth and David Smith; Marie Nightingale, Peter Loler.

THEN THERE WAS THE WEB

Searching the web for facts proved an interesting exercise, and lots of fun. I found sites such as Bricklin Society,* Duck Toller, Environment Canada, Ghosts of the Goldrush and the provincial information sites particularly useful and recommend the following for browsing:

http://www/gov.pe.ca; http://explore.gov.ns.ca; http://www.ns.ec.gc.ca/; http://www.cyber-smith.net/nbtour/; http://www/gold-rush.org/; http://www.outdoorns.com/rarebreed.html; http://www.halifax.cbc.ca/irving/default.html.

* at the time of writing the Bricklin Society sites were down.